ANGEL FACE

ANGEL FACE

The True Story of Student Killer
AMANDA KNOX

BARBIE LATZA NADEAU

BEAST BOOKS

New York

For all victims of sex crimes

Published by Beast Books
Beast Books is a co-publishing venture with the Perseus Books Group

Books published by Beast Books are available at special discounts for bulk purchases in the United States by corporations, institutions, and other organizations. For more information, please contact the Special Markets Department at the Perseus Books Group, 2300 Chestnut Street, Suite 200, Philadelphia, PA 19103, or call (800) 810-4145, ext. 5000, or e-mail special.markets@perseusbooks.com.

Editorial production by Marrathon Production Services, www.marrathon.net

DESIGN BY JANE RAESE

Library of Congress Cataloging-in-Publication Data is available.

ISBN 978-0-9842951-3-5

10 9 8 7 6 5 4 3 2

Contents

Foreword

By Tina Brown, Editor-in-Chief of *The Daily Beast*

"IT'S SUCH A SHOCK to send your child to school and for them to not come back."

That was the brokenhearted testimony of the mother of Meredith Kercher, the twenty-two-year-old British student killed in Perugia, Italy, in November 2007, at the trial of her daughter's alleged killers two years later. "We will never, never get over it."

As the mother of a nineteen-year-old myself, I shuddered at her words.

Hers is the nightmare that haunts every parent who sends a son or daughter off to one of the "gap year" or study-abroad programs that have become a right of passage for educated Western youth. But the rapid growth of such programs can be credited, in part, to parents' woeful—or is it willful?—ignorance about what can happen when students suddenly find themselves in a foreign land, free from parental or college oversight, and surrounded by a new set of peers, all of them eager to experiment.

The picturesque Umbrian hill town of Perugia may have seemed an idyllic setting for cultural and linguistic enhancement. But for the kids who signed up to go, its greater attraction was its reputation as Party Central. The lengthy official and unofficial investigations into the minds and mores of Meredith's accused killers — her fun-loving American roommate, Amanda Knox, and Knox's onetime Italian boyfriend, Raffaele Sollecito — exposed a merciless culture of sex, drugs, and alcohol that was a chilling eye-opener to parents who learned of it too late. Only with Meredith's horrific death did it become clear that she and her roommate had been mixing with a crowd that was headed not just for trouble, but, in Amanda's case, a descent into evil.

Who was Amanda Knox? Was she a fresh-faced honor student from Seattle who met anyone's definition of an all-American girl — attractive, athletic, smart, hard-working, adventuresome, in love with languages and travel? Or was her pretty face a mask, a duplicitous cover for a depraved soul? Even when all the facts of the case seem to point so tellingly in her direction, how and why could Amanda, apparently without motive, have helped slash her roommate's throat with the aid of her boyfriend and a seedy drug dealer—and then gone on to repeatedly lie about the events of that terrible autumn night?

These questions obsessed all those involved with this case, from the legal professionals to the journalists and spectators who packed the Perugia courtroom for the trial. To the Italian prosecutors and the British tabloid press, she was a drug- and sex-obsessed vixen. To her family and her defenders in the American press, she was a wholesome coed framed by an aggressive and incompetent prosecutor—or, at worst, led astray by a dissolute Italian boyfriend and the drug dealer Rudy Guede, who had gone on the lam in Germany immediately after the crime.

At *The Daily Beast*, we were fortunate, early on, to recruit the most diligent and talented English-speaking journalist covering this case.

Barbie Latza Nadeau, who has been reporting from Italy for *Newsweek* since 1997, arrived in Perugia the day after Meredith's battered body was discovered in the house she shared with three other girls. A resident of Rome, fluent in Italian, Nadeau (who also happened to have been married in Knox's hometown of Seattle) was uniquely suited to grasp all the factual and cultural nuances of this confounding case.

And she pursued them zealously. Over the next two years, she attended almost every session of Knox's murder trial, read the entire ten-thousand-page legal dossier in Italian, and invested countless coffees, dinners, and glasses of prosecco in cultivating cops, lawyers, judges, witnesses, jurors, friends, and families. Nadeau's regular posts on *The Daily Beast* during the eleven-month trial established her as an authoritative voice on the case—with appearances on CNN, CBS, NPR, the BBC, and NBC's *Dateline.* But her pieces also got her blackballed by the Knox family because she declined to toe the line they force-fed to a U.S. media eager to get them on-camera: that Amanda was a total innocent railroaded by a rogue prosecutor in a corrupt justice system.

Daily Beast readers knew otherwise, thanks to Nadeau's thorough and balanced reporting. But her objective dispatches also earned her the enmity of ferocious pro-Knox bloggers, who hurled insults and threats, hoping to discredit her professionally. Instead, her reputation has been enhanced by her diligent pursuit of a story that most of the U.S. media, including the *New York Times*, badly misread.

Barbie Latza Nadeau's sensitive, clear-eyed, and compelling examination of a perplexing case is now a

book—the second in our provocative Beast Book series—that brings to American readers the first full account of this baffling case. The book finally gets
behind the impassive "angel face" (as the Italian tabs
sneeringly called the defendant) to find the real
Amanda Knox. Mining diaries, social networking sites,
exclusive interviews, and telling moments in the courtroom, Nadeau paints the first full portrait of a quirky
young woman who is neither the "she-devil" presented
to an Italian jury nor the blameless ingenue her parents believe her to be. What Nadeau shows is that
Amanda Knox is, in fact, a twenty-first-century all-
American girl—a serious student with plans and pas-
sions—but is also a thrill-seeking young woman who
loves sex and enjoys drugs and who, in the wrong envi-
ronment with the wrong people, develops a dark side
that takes her over and tips her into the abyss.

In short, every parent's worst fear . . .

A Note on the Sources

MOST OF THE MATERIAL in this book comes directly from official court materials, which are available only in Italian. All references to forensic evidence are based on the transcripts of court testimony and the ten-thousand-page crime dossier known as the Digital Archive. The archive includes police reports, photos, and most of the interrogation transcripts, as well as Amanda Knox's and Raffaele Sollecito's prison writings and intercepts of their visiting-room conversations. I also refer to PowerPoint presentations, slide shows, and other exhibits presented in court by key witnesses for both the prosecution and the defense. Rudy Guede's testimony comes from interviews with his lawyers and official transcripts of both his fast-track and his appellate trials. The rest of the information about the trial was garnered by my attendance at every session of the eleven-month trial of Knox and Sollecito, except for two sessions in mid-June 2009. In addition, I viewed roughly ten hours of video taken during the crime scene investigation and listened to audiotapes of Amanda's and Raffaele's interrogations in prison and the Skype call to Rudy Guede in Germany. Amanda and Raffaele's MySpace quotes and Amanda's short stories come from downloads of their MySpace pages made before this material was removed from the Internet in 2007. I obtained Amanda's personal e-mails to friends through sources in Seattle.

I first arrived in Perugia on November 3, 2007, the day after Meredith Kercher's body was discovered. I was on assignment for *Newsweek*. Over the next two years, I became personally acquainted with the prosecutors and lawyers on all sides of the complex case mounted against Knox and Sollecito and the simpler fast-track prosecution of Guede. I interviewed the principal players in both cases several times and often videotaped the interviews, which resulted in more than twenty hours of exclusive footage pertinent to the case. Unless otherwise attributed, quotes from Edda Mellas, Curt Knox, and the Sollecito family come from formal interviews and informal conversations throughout 2008 and 2009. Comments from the jurors come from interviews I conducted with them soon after the verdict in December 2009. Quotes from the lawyers and prosecutors are from text messages, e-mail exchanges, formal interviews, and informal conversations in Rome, in Florence, in the halls of the court-house, and on the streets of Perugia. I spoke to all these attorneys frequently in various settings; Perugia is a small town where all sides involved in Italy's "trial of the century" were constantly crossing paths.

I also made a valuable friend in Italo Carmignani, a seasoned crime reporter for *Il Messaggero* with great local contacts; he generously shared his exclusive knowledge of the case. In addition, I did extensive interviewing in Perugia among the students familiar with the social scene in 2007 and traveled to Seattle in the summer of 2008 to investigate Amanda's background. Andrea Vogt of the *Seattle Post Intelligencer*, who is based in Bologna, shared photos of Amanda's neighborhood and schools in Seattle.

Finally, I traveled frequently to Florence in 2009 to attend court sessions in the abuse-of-office case against Giuliano Mignini, the lead prosecutor in the Knox trial.

Cast of Characters

THE VICTIM

Meredith Kercher, student

THE CONVICTED

Rudy Guede, local drifter
Amanda Knox, student
Raffaele Sollecito, student

THE ACCUSED

Patrick Lumumba, bar owner

THE JUDGE

Giancarlo Massei, decided case with second judge

THE PROSECUTION

Monica Napoleoni, head of Perugia's homicide squad
Giuliano Mignini, co-prosecutor for Knox and
Sollecito

Manuela Comodi, co-prosecutor
Patrizia Stefanoni, forensic specialist

THE DEFENSE

Valter Biscotti, lawyer for Rudy Guede
Giulia Bongiorno, lead lawyer for Raffaele Sollecito
Carlo Dalla Vedova, lead lawyer for Amanda Knox
Luciano Ghirga, local lawyer for Amanda Knox
David Marriott, Knox family spokesman

THE FAMILIES

Curt Knox, Amanda's father
Edda Mellas, Amanda's mother
Chris Mellas, Amanda's stepfather
Deanna Knox, Amanda's sister
John Kercher, Meredith's father
Arline Kercher, Meredith's mother
Francesco Sollecito, Raffaele's father

1

"Perugia Is Not for the Weak"

IT IS 2 A.M. on a sticky September night, and Perugia is a cauldron of illicit activity. A thick fog of marijuana hangs over the Piazza IV Novembre. Empty bottles and plastic cups litter the cobbled square. The periphery is lined with North African drug dealers, selling their wares like the fruit vendors who occupy this spot in daytime hours. A group of pretty young British students giggle, easy prey to the Italian guys pouring their drinks. The American girls are more aggressive, eager to nab an Italian lover. Down an alley, a young man has lifted the skirt of his conquest and is having clumsy sex with her under a streetlamp while her drink spills out of the plastic cup in her hand. Dozens of students are passed out on the steps of the church. There is not a cop in sight.

This is the scene that greets the study-abroad crowd when they enroll at Perugia's universities for foreigners. It comes as a shock to some and an irresistible circus to others, and it was the backdrop for tragedy in the case of two young women, Amanda Marie Knox, then twenty, and Meredith Susana Cara Kercher, twenty-two, who arrived in the fall of 2007 and enthusiastically joined the party. Less than two months later, Meredith was dead, and Amanda was in prison, accused of her murder.

These young women were not exactly innocents abroad. They had both done their share of college partying before they arrived in Italy. But that was hardly preparation for the nonstop bacchanalia that has made Perugia infamous on the international student circuit. Tina Rocchio is the Italy coordinator of Arcadia University, which facilitates many study-abroad trips. "When they want to go to Perugia, my first question is always, 'How much self-discipline do they have?' before I can recommend it," she says. "Perugia is not for the weak. The students who go there are of two veins — either they party or they study, and Perugia usually means a party."

In the 1920s, Benito Mussolini established universities for foreigners in Perugia and nearby Siena, aiming to spread Italy's "superior culture" around the world by recruiting foreigners to study cheaply in these lovely, walled cities. The Siena school remains relatively small. But the school in Perugia, in tandem with the city's Università degli Studi, which also caters to foreigners but has a larger contingent of Italians, spawned dozens of smaller satellite campuses. There are so many that the town's student population is now roughly 40,000, around a quarter of the city's total population of 163,000. Perugia is popular among foreign students looking for something cheaper and cozier than Paris, Barcelona, or Florence, these last three cities being the top choices for well-heeled Americans. The academic offerings are wide-ranging, and the professors have a reputation for being forgiving. Sometimes, the college credits transfer back home as a simple pass-fail mark, when they should actually be given a grade-point score. All this attracts an eclectic mix of young people from around the globe. Most of the Italian kids come from wealthy families; in Italy, university students usually live at home, and it is a rare privilege to go away to school. The foreign students— the universities are accredited in Asia, Europe, and North America—are more likely to be scraping by on scholarships and second jobs. With very few dorm rooms available, the students usually live in the historic center in flophouses and apartments that have been partitioned into tiny rooms to accommodate multiple renters. The town is full of discos, clubs, and cheap restaurants that cater to a student clientele.

No surprise, Perugia is also a drug dealer's paradise; the mostly North African merchants do a lively trade in everything from genetically modified hashish to cocaine and acid. It is very easy to get high in Perugia, and the police generally turn a blind eye. Perugia has a very low crime rate compared with the rest of Italy. Despite its reputation, drug arrests are rare, and the police are routinely lenient with the student population. The narrow, cobbled streets, some of which are built in steps, discourage car use, so the students stagger around the city center on foot, and the drunk driving offenses that usually dominate college-town crime dockets are not a problem. Murders are extremely rare—with one notable exception. The year before Meredith was killed, another young woman, Sonia Marra, who was studying medicine at the Università degli Studi, disappeared without a trace. The body has never been found, and it was only recently that her former boyfriend was arrested in connection with her murder—amid suspicions that the investigation into her death was neglected during the two-year circus following Meredith's murder.

Perugia was home to the famous artist Pietro Vannucci, who went on to teach Renaissance great Raphael. It is also famous for the Perugina chocolate factory, now owned by Nestlé. But without the universities, Perugia would be just another postcard-perfect Umbrian hill town competing for the tourist dollar with Siena, Assisi, and St. Gimagnano. The local community looks askance at the wild student culture, but also knows better than to interfere much with the town's economic mainstay. As one Perugian prosecutor told a reporter, with long-suffering tolerance, "This kind of intoxicating freedom gets into these kids so far away from home, this total lack of control, this hunger for experience rules these kids." The universities and administrators of study-abroad programs contribute immensely to Perugia, and they expect the local community to be forgiving. They insist, too, that the party scene is no worse here than any other college town.

Meredith Kercher came to Perugia from the University of Leeds. Established in 1904 by King Edward VII as an alternative to elitist Oxford and Cambridge, Leeds promised access to all. Today, there are roughly thirty thousand students on the campus, where buildings from the 1960s are interlaced with glass walkways and structures more modern. The academic program is serious, far-reaching, and international-minded. In her two years there, studying European politics, Meredith proved herself an exceptional student with a quick grasp of languages, and she was accepted into the prestigious European Region Action Scheme for the Mobility of University Students. Known as ERASMUS, the program was established by the European Commission in 1994 to facilitate international study; its goal is to have three million students and teachers in active exchange programs in thirty-two countries by 2012. But the ERASMUS program also has a reputation for fun. At any of the participating universities, the ERASMUS parties are reputed to be the most multicultural and exciting.

Meredith was a slender woman with pretty features that reflected her mixed heritage; her father is British, her mother an Indian born in Lahore when Pakistan was still considered part of confederated India. The young woman's background, according to her hometown newspaper in Croydon, South London, was "solid, very proper middle-upper class." She was a typical British girl who had her fair share of romances and who was not particularly embarrassed about being sloppy drunk in public—she had been stopped once for public intoxication with friends in Leeds. She had three boyfriends in her two years at Leeds. Her latest beau was the most serious, but the two decided amicably to calm things down before she went to study in Perugia and he in Australia.

Meredith's father, John Kercher, then sixty-four, worked for the British tabloids as a sort of print paparazzo. In the 1980s, he followed celebs around town and hobnobbed backstage at concerts. At the height of his career, twenty years ago, he wrote pop culture annuals for the teen set on Michael Jackson, Madonna, Culture Club, A-Ha, and Wham. He also wrote snap biographies of Warren Beatty and Joan Collins. John worked hard, and the Kercher family lived well. Meredith and her three siblings attended an expensive and prestigious high school called Croydon Old Palace School, where Meredith was treasured for her upbeat personality. "She would come downstairs in the morning and start dancing in front of everyone and it made us all laugh," her sister later told reporters. "She was so much fun and had a wicked sense of humor."

Amanda Knox, too, was both a dedicated scholar and, like most American coeds, an accomplished party girl. Back in Seattle, she was a linguist who dreamed of being a writer. She had an insatiable appetite for reading, often simultaneously devouring the same books in multiple languages. She was reading *Harry Potter* in German at the time of her arrest, and her parents say she had considered becoming a journalist. She defined herself on her social networking pages as a "peaceful partier," and her only brush with the law was a disturbing-the-peace arrest for a house party she threw. Seattle is not so different from Leeds. It is a liberal U.S. city, with a diverse demographic. The Seattle area hosts some big hitters such as Boeing, which was founded there, and Microsoft in nearby Redmond, but the area is equally well known for spawning grunge music and Starbucks coffee. The youth population prides itself on being avant-garde, but the prevailing culture is wholesome, outdoorsy, free.

Amanda's parents, Curt Knox, forty-nine, and Edda Mellas, forty-seven, split up when she was just a few years old, and she spent her childhood shuffling between their homes. Edda raised her, but Curt was involved in her life even as he built a new family with his second wife, Cassandra, forty-six. Curt worked as a manager at Macy's, and Edda was an elementary-school librarian who then switched to teaching math to boost her income. Seattle is expensive and money was tight; Amanda was far from spoiled. She won a partial scholarship for the prestigious Seattle Preparatory School, a private Jesuit high school, where she excelled both academically and socially. Kent Hickey, president of Seattle Prep, never waivered in his support of her. "This is an extremely unusual situation," Hickey told the *Seattle Times.* "A lot of people said 'don't get involved,' but we can't sit this out. This is really important and we can't pick and choose the graduates we help."

Amanda had an appetite for travel from a young age. After studying Japanese her freshman year in high school, she spent a few weeks with a Japanese family as part of a student exchange program. Upon graduating, she went on to the University of Washington, where she studied German, Italian, and creative writing. She worked her way through college slinging coffee and taking orders at a fine-arts frame shop and saved up seven thousand dollars to study abroad—which was barely enough to afford a semester in Perugia.

In the United States, the "angel face" that would grace dozens of Italian magazine covers was not such a standout. Amanda's looks were close to the norm in Seattle, although her quirky personality and sense of humor quickly endeared her to friends. In Italy, her blue eyes and even features were slightly exotic, and she soon highlighted her dishwater blond hair to match her Italian roommates' and pierced her ears a few more times to fit into the Perugia scene. She hadn't had many boyfriends in Seattle. Her true love was David Johnsrud, twenty-two, a student at the University of Washington known as DJ, with whom she rock-climbed and partied, but she often complained to friends that he stopped short of having sex with her. When lurid speculation about sex games began to swirl around Meredith's murder, DJ told a British documentary filmmaker that "speaking personally and speaking to many of the other friends, we've never heard Amanda express any interest in that sort of group orgy thing."

Unlike Meredith, who enrolled in the Università degli Studi to complete a rigorous European studies program, Amanda did not come to Perugia as part of a structured exchange program. She devised her own independent study plan and enrolled in a hodgepodge of courses in German, Italian, and creative writing at the Università per Stranieri. Her semester abroad had no real supervision beyond an e-mail address for the University of Washington's office of International Programs and Exchanges. As a twenty-year-old, she was not even old enough to legally drink in the United States. In Perugia, no one cared what she did.

In August 2007, Amanda arrived in Europe with ambitious plans. First she and her younger sister Deanna Knox, then eighteen, flew from Seattle to Hamburg, to visit their aunt, Dorothy Craft Najir. Amanda's mom had been born in Germany and moved to the United States at the age of six, so Amanda was curious to see where she and her *oma*, or grandmother, had lived. After a few days tooling around Germany and Austria with their aunt and uncle, the Knox sisters flew to Milan and then hopped a train down to Perugia by way of Florence. On her September 2, 2007, MySpace page, Amanda wrote,

> from munich deanna and i flew off to italy together.
> landed in milan took a train to florence (on the way we
> met frederico, an italian guy who doesnt speak english).

She later wrote in a personal e-mail to a friend that she had sex with him in the bathroom of the train. She elaborated on the same September 2 MySpace entry:

> in fact, met a guy named frederico on the train to
> florence from milan, and we ended up hanging out
> together in florence, where he bought both deanna and
> i dinner and then, when deanna went to bed, we smoked
> up together, my first time in italy . . .

In Perugia, the sisters searched the classifieds and
message boards for an apartment. Amanda's uncle had
lined up a two-week internship at the Bundestag to kick-
start her German studies, and she was planning to return
to Perugia after she finished in Berlin. But she wanted
to sew up her living arrangements in advance. She
found the house on via della Pergola by pure chance:

> i need to find a place to live, so i search desperately
> through italian classifieds. i also buy a phone. then,
> when we walk down a steep road to my university, we
> run into a very skinny girl who looks a little older than
> me putting up a page with her number on the outer wall
> of the unversity. i chat it up with her, she speaks english
> really well, and we go immediately to her place, literally
> 2minutes walk from my university.

Indeed, Filomena Romanelli, then twenty-eight,
was hoping for someone just like Amanda to take one

of the back bedrooms in the apartment she and her friend Laura Mezzetti, then twenty-seven, were renting. The two Italian women worked as legal assistants at a nearby law firm. Both Filomena and Laura liked to smoke pot, and Filomena had a serious boyfriend. Laura, on the other hand, once confided to Amanda that she had bedded the washing machine repairman in desperation. *"Forza* Laura—you go girl!" Amanda wrote of the story on her MySpace pages. But not long after, Laura found a boyfriend with whom she spent most nights. The Italian women sublet rooms at the villa to make ends meet. Renting to foreign students was also a good way to practice their English, and the young tenants would never stay for long. It was a strange house, once an outbuilding in an old farmstead, that seemed to hang off the side of the hill just below the city's fortress wall. It felt remote, but it was actually just tucked out of sight. The busy street called via Sant'Antonio was parallel with the rooftop, yet the villa was impossible to see unless you knew it was there.

The house was L-shaped, with a covered portico at the front that opened into a tiny foyer where the girls hung keys, parked umbrellas, and kept a bulletin board with messages to each other. The foyer opened

into the apartment's one common area—a live-in
kitchen that had been cheaply renovated and filled
with IKEA furniture, tattered sofas and a green
Formica table. Laura and Filomena had hung fabric
on the walls and put down colorful rugs to brighten up
the dismal space. Their bedrooms were off this living
area at the front of the house, and they shared the
larger bathroom next to the kitchen. The sublet rooms
were down a short corridor to the back of the house.
The hallway gave onto a small terrace and ended at a
bare-bones bathroom with a flimsy Plexiglas shower
stall. Meredith, arriving first, took the corner room,
and Amanda was left with the smaller one next door.
Both these rooms were tiny, with just enough space for
a single bed, a small closet, and a writing desk. Downstairs, four young Italian men shared an apartment
with a similar layout but far less light.

Amanda loved the place.

it's a cute house that is right in the middle of this
random garden int he middle of perugia. around us are
apartment buildings, but we enter through a gate and
there it is. im in love. i meet her roommate. . . . the
house has a kitchen, 2 bathrooms, and four bathrooms
[sic] not to mention a washing maschine, and internet

access. not to mention, she owns two guitars and wants to play with me. not to mention the view is amazing. not to mention i have a terrace that looks over the perugian city/countryside. not to mention she wants me to teach erh yoga. not to mention they both smoke like chimneys. and, she offers me one of the open rooms after we hang out for a bit. we exchange numbers. i put down a down payment. im feeling sky high. these girls are awesome. really sweet, really down to earth, funny as hell. neither are students, they actually both work int he same law office, and they are desperate for roommates because the two they had decided they wanted to disappear all of a sudden. they are relieved to meet me believe it or not, because aparently everyone else they have met have been really not cool.

Her rent was three hundred euros a month, which is steep by Perugia standards, but Amanda didn't care. She had seen worse places for more money, and she was just relieved to find a place to settle.

fuck that. im hooked. we hung out for a good long time the day before yesturday, just laughing about crazy people and in general getting to know each other. then, deanna and i went to grab a sandwich at the same cafe and i bumped into the most beautiful black man i have ever seen. he said he'd see me when i come back from germany. eheheheh and our waiter, nerti, from albania, hung out with us a bit and talked politics.

After paying a deposit and signing the lease, Amanda went to Berlin, and Deanna went home to Seattle. But after a few days at the Bundestag, things went wrong. Amanda walked out on her internship, leaving her uncle in the awkward situation of explaining why his American niece gave up such a hard-to-get opportunity. Her MySpace page on September 15, 2007, offers little real explanation:

i was in the way and they didnt need me there anyway. i called in the next morning and that was that. then i walked, and walked and walked and walked. all over berlin, for two whole days. it was great. i was supposed to pick up a bus on friday, so i spent wednesday and thursday wandering around berlin, seeing things, meeting people, drinking a glass of wine in a park near my apartment every night. fantastic. then i got back home to hamburg and found out i was in trouble with my uncle who ahd landed me the job at the bundestag in the first place. aparently he had to go to a lot of

trouble to get me my spot there and everyone was
confused as to what had happened to me. so i talked to
him today and explain ed the mess, but not before
freaking out and crying a little becaue i was afraid i
made my uncle look bad in front of these very importan
people. oops. to say the least.

Meanwhile, Meredith Kercher was planning her
own Perugian adventure. As part of the ERASMUS
program, she had more structure to her academic life
and a built-in network of friends, but she had chosen
to live on her own, instead of with a sponsor family or
in a supervised dormitory. She, too, went to Perugia in
late August looking for a place to live. She called a
couple of places before finding the notice that Filomena had hung up the same day she met Amanda.
Meredith, called "Mez" by close friends, already spoke
good Italian and wanted to live in the community to
hone her language skills. She moved into one of the
back bedrooms before Amanda Knox returned from
Germany.

The two Anglophone girls were instant friends.
They spent a lot of time together in the first weeks and
often stayed up late chatting about their lives and
loves. But they were in different programs at different

schools, so their circles began to diverge once Meredith started classes. She attended the ERASMUS orientation events and parties; Amanda found it hard to meet people. Meredith tried to include her housemate in gatherings with her new British friends, but Amanda didn't fit in. They were put off by her loud voice and the way she always tried to be the center of attention. In the middle of a conversation, she would start singing at the top of her voice. The British girls were a far cry from her Seattle crowd, and Amanda seemed rough and crude to them. She spent a lot of time at Internet cafés and playing her guitar on the tiny terrace. She also realized she didn't have enough money to carry her through the semester, so she started looking for work. Within a few days, she found a job at Le Chic, a funky reggae bar owned by Congolese immigrant Patrick Lumumba, forty-four.

Within a month, the relationship that began so warmly between two girls far from home had soured into the sort of chronic, low-level irritation that often afflicts roommates. The mystery that has riveted two continents since November 2, 2007—when Meredith's slashed and battered body was found in their shared flat—was how and why the relationship deteriorated rapidly to the point of extreme violence. How is

it possible that two well-brought-up young women became parties to such a grisly crime? What actually
went on that night? Who is the real Amanda Knox behind the inscrutable mask she presented in court—the
wholesome innocent described by her family or the
heartless seductress portrayed in the most lurid media
accounts? After a year of intense investigation, eleven
months of trial, and three murder convictions, answering those questions still involves a certain amount of
speculation. But the more one knows about the evidence in the case—much of it overlooked in U.S.
press accounts—the easier it is to understand how
these young women fell prey to the temptations of Perugia, with tragic results.

2

"Here Is the List of People I've Had Sex With"

TWO MONTHS BEFORE Meredith Kercher moved to Perugia, she made a sultry appearance in a music video, sauntering down a dark spiral stairway as Kristian Leontiou sings "Some Say." The song is bubblegum pop, and the video, in which a number of pretty young women dance under falling petals, is amateurish and low-budget. But the lyrics are haunting, given that the video was released on October 24, 2007, one week before Meredith was murdered. "No more trouble in my soul, no more time to make me whole."

Leontiou was not well known, and the video went largely unnoticed until two years later, when Meredith's parents drew press attention to it during her murder trial. This was part of a calculated effort to remind the public, judge, and jury that their daughter was a vibrant, beautiful young woman, not a one-dimensional crime victim. Up to then, Meredith had been known primarily through two photos—one in a gray tank top with a smiling face, the other made up as a vampire for Halloween the night before her death, with fake blood on her chin. In the fourteen months between her death and the murder trial, public attention focused almost exclusively on the accused, Amanda Knox, the enigmatic All-American beauty who seemed such an unlikely killer.

The music video momentarily turned the spotlight back onto Meredith. (When the video became popular online, Amanda's most ardent supporters tried to discredit it by claiming that the girl in the clip was not Meredith; Leontiou eventually confirmed that it was.) But the release of the video also highlighted a sensual side of her at odds with the prosecution's theory of the case. She had, since her murder, been portrayed as a somewhat prissy British girl who was scandalized and intimidated by her roommate's aggressive sexuality. In reality, though, Meredith was hardly a prude.

"She was no angel," her family's lawyer, Francesco Maresca, fifty, once told me at his office in Florence. "She was simply a young woman of her time. She had more than one boyfriend. She was normal."

When she arrived in Perugia, Meredith behaved like most of the other students, reveling in the freedom of being so far from home. She hadn't broken up with her boyfriend back at Leeds University, Patrick Cronin, then twenty-three, and in fact was wearing a pair of his blue jeans when she was killed. But they had decided to loosen their ties while they both studied abroad, and she quickly became interested in a young man who lived in the basement apartment on via della Pergola. Giacomo Silenzi, twenty-two, was a long-haired, earring-wearing student from the Marche region in eastern Italy. He played guitar in a band and was well known around town as a party guy. Meredith met him in early September, when she first moved into the house, and both she and Amanda had been to his apartment to smoke pot on more than one occasion. It was in the downstairs apartment that both girls met Rudy Guede, twenty-three, an Ivory Coast immigrant who had come to Italy as a child. Whenever the guys downstairs needed hashish or marijuana, they called Rudy, who often stayed on to enjoy the party. Rudy had once gotten so high that he fell asleep on the toilet. Giacomo's roommate found him there with his pants around his ankles in the morning.

Giacomo and Meredith began sleeping together

about ten days before her death, and Giacomo admitted that they had gone as far as experimenting with anal sex, which Meredith didn't like. Meredith's friends remember that she was upset when Amanda confided that she liked Giacomo, too, but then said, "You can have him." Giacomo later said he never liked Amanda, and he was one of the first witnesses to suggest, during police interviews, that Amanda was involved in the murder.

Meredith and Amanda were not the polar opposites later described by prosecutors. They were both smart, studious young women whose good grades came easily. They both loved to read and engage in deep, searching conversations. They were often described in the same way by their friends back home, who spoke of their beauty, sense of humor, wit, and charm. Moreover, both Amanda and Meredith liked to smoke the occasional joint, get drunk, and flirt. And both women were fully aware of their sexual power.

Their family backgrounds were also similar in some ways. The two women were children of divorce. Meredith had grown up in the heart of multicultural England, in Coulsdon, South London, and remained in contact with both parents. She and her sister Stephanie and two brothers, Lyle and John, formed a close-knit family that was protective of their mother, Arline Kercher, who suffers from diabetes-related illnesses. When she came to Perugia, Meredith kept her British cell phone active so that her mother could always reach her in an emergency; Meredith borrowed a second phone, for local calls, from her new roommate Filomena. The English student had already bought her plane ticket to be home for her mother's birthday on December 19 and stashed a gift of Perugina chocolates in her suitcase under the bed.

Amanda was also close to her mother and younger sister Deanna. The three even got matching tattoos of a yellow flower on the backs of their necks just before Amanda left for Europe. Amanda's parents divorced when Amanda was two years old and Edda was pregnant with Deanna. Edda eventually married Chris Mellas, a tech consultant twelve years her junior, and Amanda grew up in the lower-middle-class White Center neighborhood in West Seattle, where the neighbors' yards are littered with rusty cars. Her father, Curt, married his mistress, Cassandra, and lived in a nicer, middle-class district about half a mile away. Amanda was close to her two younger half-sisters, Ashley and Delaney, but somewhat jealous of them, too. She called them "the replacement children."

Amanda's relationship with her stepfather was strained, according to friends in Seattle, who say that Amanda and Chris competed for Edda's love. Amanda was fourteen when her thirty-nine-year-old mother fell in love with Chris, then twenty-seven—that is, about equally close in age to mother and daughter. Eventually, friends say, Chris and Amanda became drinking partners, and they often argued. On August 21, 2007, at 2:38 A.M., Amanda sent a post from Perugia to Chris's MySpace page, "hahaha alright, does that mean we're getting along then? happy birthday loser."

Chris's own entry on MySpace read:

> About my life: I am married, happily, and I have two kids by marriage, Amanda and Deanna. They are both shitheads and I love them anyways. Deanna is a senior now in HS and Amanda is on her second year in college. They are both cool. They, as we all do, have their fair share of quirks . . . but we would all be white bread boring as hell if we didn't.

The crucial difference between the new roommates on via della Pergola was that Amanda was unusually bold about her sexuality, while Meredith retained a certain modesty. There was no clothes dryer in their apartment, only a rack in the hallway, where Meredith was reluctant to hang her panties, and she was offended when Amanda left a clear plastic cosmetics case containing condoms and a vibrator in their shared bathroom. Not long after they moved in together, the two young women went out to the Red Zone discotheque, where they met up by chance with Giacomo and his friend Daniel de Luna, a twenty-two-year-old student from Rome who often came to Perugia to visit the guys downstairs. They all danced and flirted. Giacomo kissed Meredith for the first time on the dance floor, and she later confided to her British friends that this was romantic and "very Italian" and that she hoped it was the prelude to a more intimate relationship. Amanda and Daniel connected more quickly; he would later brag to friends that he ended up in her room that night having sex.

After she was arrested, the police set a trap for Amanda by telling her she had tested positive for HIV. This sort of psychological trickery is commonly used by investigators in Italy to illicit a confession. In this case, it led a terrified Amanda to make a grave error that would permanently taint her image. She listed all the men she had slept with recently, trying to decide who might have infected her. The prosecutors knew the press would jump at these salacious details of Amanda's sex life, and one of the detectives close to the case leaked the document to British tabloid reporter Nick Pisa, who broke the story. Amanda wrote in her prison diary:

> I don't want to die. I want to get married and have children. I want to create something good. I want to get old. I want my time. I want my life. Why why why? I can't believe this. I don't know where I could have got HIV from. Here is the list of people I've had sex with in Italy [scratched out and replaced with] in general:
>
> 1. Kyle—also a virgin
> 2. James—checks regularly and always used a condom
> 3. Ross—a one-night stand, pull out
> 4. DJ—condoms, mom is a nurse, he would know
> 5. Elis—pull out—one night stand
> 6. Daniele [sic]—condoms, one night stand
> 7. Raffaele—condoms, one time w/o

At the end, she concluded that it had to be Ross, Elis, or Raffaele Sollecito, then twenty-three, her most recent conquest, who, she noted, "used to use extensive drugs." (Police later told Amanda that the test results had been a "false positive.")

Consensual sex is not a crime. So Amanda's promiscuity has little bearing on the murder itself. But her uninhibited behavior did cause problems between the roommates—problems that the prosecution would try to spin into a motive for murder. In his final arguments, the lead prosecutor hypothesized that as Amanda helped assault Meredith, she yelled, "You are always behaving like a little saint. Now we will show you. Now we will make you have sex." Even before coming to Europe, Amanda, at times, seemed obsessed with sex. The to-do list she made for moving to Perugia included visiting a sex shop and buying condoms. Her diaries were full of fantasy letters to various lovers. To one former boyfriend she wrote in August 2007: "I'm waiting for you, I want to see something porno with you and put it into practice with you." And once she arrived in Europe, she e-mailed friends back home about hooking up with a stranger on the train. One of her last postings on Facebook declared, "I don't get embarrassed and therefore have very few social inhibitions."

Sexual confidence is one thing; blatant exhibitionism is quite another. Meredith was so mortified by the pink "Rampant Rabbit" vibrator on display in their shared bathroom that she felt compelled to point it out to everyone who visited and explain that it wasn't hers. It almost seemed as if Amanda were brandishing it as a symbol of her sexual power over Meredith. "Isn't it odd that a girl arrives and the first thing she shows is a vibrator?" Meredith's friend Amy Frost would later ask.

Housekeeping was another point of conflict among the roommates. Amanda left unwashed dishes in the kitchen, her clothes and shoes were often scattered throughout the common areas, and Filomena and Laura finally resorted to a cleaning schedule in an effort to keep the house tidy. Meredith was especially disgusted by the fact that Amanda rarely flushed or scoured the toilet. But that issue may have been in part cultural. Back home in Seattle, over-flushing is an ecological faux pas. "If it's yellow let it mellow. If it's brown flush it down," goes the popular West Coast mantra. That brand of eco-vigilance is not part of the British psyche, however, and Meredith felt that Amanda was leaving the toilet dirty intentionally to offend her. She complained about it to her parents.

As is so often the case in university life, fast friendships die even more quickly than they form. Amanda and Meredith were very close when Amanda first moved in. But the bond quickly withered, and everyone in the household soon grew wary of Amanda, who persisted in bringing home a parade of strangers even when the other girls asked her to stop. In Perugia, all sorts of young and not-so-young men lurk on the edges of the student scene, ever ready to make a drug connection or exploit some foreign girl's romantic fantasies about life in Italy. Amanda did not always bring these men back for sex, although she did manage to bed a Greek, an Albanian, and an Italian other than Raffaele during her first few weeks in Perugia. Still, she was trusting and naive with strangers in a way that made the other roommates feel increasingly vulnerable. They worried that Amanda would bring home someone who would rape or rob them. Meredith was particularly concerned about an Argentinean man whom Amanda had met at an Internet café. He was too friendly, often touching and kissing both Amanda and Meredith against their will. Meredith told friends how uncomfortable she was about him coming to the house, and they, in turn, would tell police that the Argentinean was most likely her killer. But he was out of town when the murder occurred.

A few days after Meredith and Giacomo started their romantic relationship, on October 25, 2007,

Amanda met Raffaele Sollecito at a classical music concert. She was drawn to him immediately because he looked like Harry Potter, with his wire-rim glasses and boyish face. Raffaele was the son of a successful urologist in the southern city of Bari. The doctor was well-connected and treated the Pugliese elite; he showed up at court with an entourage that included bodyguards and a driver for his armored car. Raf was both spoiled and dominated by his father and had ready access to money with which to bankroll a penchant for drugs. While many of the other students in Perugia shared cramped rooms and slept on floors, Raffaele's father had set his son up with his own apartment and a regular cleaning woman.

Raffaele's mother died when he was young, and his father remarried a younger woman whose fur coats and coiffed hair with skunk highlights would become fodder for many pressroom jokes during the trial. Raf was a techie who spent long hours decoding difficult problems for his degree in computer studies. At one point during his trial, he was even asked to fix the prosecutor's computer amid jokes that he might hit "delete all" when she turned her head. He also had a fascination with swords and knives. He always carried a switchblade with him and he often played with it when he was bored. He even bragged to his father that he took a knife with him when he was called in for questioning by the police.

On his Facebook page, Raf wrote about being stoned all day, enjoying "risky things," and at times being "completely crazy." He posted photos of himself in various states of a drug haze; in one, he is wrapped in surgical bandages and brandishing a meat cleaver. Although he had little experience with women for an Italian man of twenty-three—there was only one girl-friend before Amanda—he was actively, somewhat morbidly, fixated on sex. He masturbated constantly, according to many of his university acquaintances. And a counselor in his college dorm would testify to once walking in to see a "bestiality scene" on Raffaele's computer.

Amanda and Raffaele had been lovers for only one week when Meredith was killed. The relationship was fresh and passionate, but it was not monogamous for Amanda. She was still romantically linked to DJ, her old boyfriend from Seattle, and was still bedding casual acquaintances. Amanda told her Greek friend Spiros that she felt slightly guilty starting up with Raffaele when she still had feelings for DJ, who was kept in the dark about her life in Perugia even though they talked on Skype and e-mailed often. Two nights after Amanda and Raf got involved, she also hooked up once more with Daniel de Luna, the friend of her downstairs neighbors, and later included him on the list of sex partners in her prison diary. Nevertheless, Raf bragged to friends that he and Amanda were having sex three or four times a day, usually under the influence of marijuana or hashish. His father was not happy about the romance. In an intercepted phone conversation days after the murder, he told his son to "erase" Amanda from his mind. "Cancel her out." After Raffaele's arrest, his father told ABC News, "She has ruined my son's life. I damn the day he met her."

While Raf appeared to have a bottomless bank account, Amanda had always struggled to pay her own way. She worked three jobs while attending university back in Washington and scrimped to save the money for a year abroad. She worked every night but Monday at Patrick Lumumba's Le Chic bar, waiting tables and handing out flyers for the bar's events. But Patrick had been heard to complain that Amanda spent more time talking and flirting with customers than she did selling drinks. He was about to fire her and was considering hiring Meredith for her job. Amanda was scheduled to work on November 1, the night after Halloween.

Italians do not celebrate Halloween, but the next day, All Souls', is an important holiday. That's the day when the spirits of the dead come to visit the living, and family members light candles and leave flowers at the graves of their loved ones. Perugia emptied out for the long holiday weekend. Both Laura and Filomena, eager to avoid the debauchery sure to accompany the foreign students' Halloween parties, made plans to stay away. Filomena went to her boyfriend's house, and Laura went home to Viterbo. Giacomo and the guys downstairs all went home to visit the graves of their aunts, uncles, and grandparents. Both Amanda and Meredith stayed out late on Halloween. Amanda worked at Le Chic and then went to a party until 5 A.M.; Meredith party-hopped until 6:30 A.M. Amanda then went to bed at Raffaele's and returned home around 11 A.M. the next day to take a shower and change clothes. Meredith was there alone, and they chatted briefly. Amanda later recounted that Meredith's jowls were still stained with the fake blood of her vampire costume. Raffaele arrived soon after Amanda got out of the shower, and the two went off to Amanda's bedroom, where they say they had sex and took a nap.

Giacomo had left a key to the lower apartment with Meredith and asked her to look out for their adopted stray cat and water the marijuana plants he kept under fluorescent lights in a narrow hallway. Meredith studied for a few hours, trying to finish a paper that was due on Monday, and then went downstairs to water the pot. When she finished, she sent Giacomo a flirty text message saying how excited she was to see him when he got back.

Around 3 P.M., too tired to study, Meredith left via della Pergola to visit her friend Robyn Butterworth, then twenty-two. She did not say good-bye to Amanda and Raffaele, who were still in Amanda's room. Amanda and Raffaele say that an hour later, they went out for a classic *passeggiata*, the late afternoon stroll Italians take around the center of town, returning to Raffaele's before Amanda was scheduled to work at Le Chic. They had sex one more time, and then, Amanda says, she left around 8 P.M. to go home and get ready for work. At 8:18 P.M., Patrick sent Amanda a text message to tell her that business was slow and that she did not have to come in that night. She wrote back, in Italian: "*Ci vediamo più tardi. Buona serata*—We'll see you a little later. Good evening." Both Raffaele's and Amanda's cell phones were turned off around 8:30 P.M. and turned on again just after 6 A.M. the next day. Amanda would later tell police that she went back to

Raffaele's house, where they downloaded the movie *Stardust* and watched *Amélie,* made some dinner, smoked pot, and had sex. She described how they then took a shower together and how Raffaele dried her hair. But police computer technicians would determine that Raf did not download anything that night. At 8:40 P.M., his father called on the apartment's land line, but no one answered.

Meanwhile, Meredith relaxed at Robyn's house with her friends Amy Frost, then twenty-one, and Sophie Purton, then twenty. They laughed and gossiped about the night before. Then they made a pizza and an apple pie while watching *The Notebook* on DVD. At around 9 P.M., Meredith said she was tired. She and Sophie left together and split up on via Roscetto, each heading to her own house. No one knows exactly what happened next, although police would eventually gather these confusing details:

At 7:41 P.M., one of three closed-circuit TV cameras in the parking garage across from the girls' villa captured the image of a man in a heavy jacket, wearing sneakers, heading toward via della Pergola. The camera caught him leaving twenty minutes later and again, after a half hour, returning in the direction of via della Pergola. The man was clearly white, not black, but defense attorneys for both Raffaele and Amanda would later insist that this was Rudy Guede. At 8:43 P.M., the same video shows a woman in a white skirt—the prosecutor would claim that the woman was Amanda—heading home. Antonio Curatolo, then fifty-one, is a homeless man who spends his time on a bench by the Piazza Grimana basketball courts near the via della Pergola. He testified that he saw Amanda and Raffaele looking down toward the gate of the house around 9:30 P.M. He said they returned to the Piazza Grimana again at 10:30 and stood looking down over the railing toward Amanda and Meredith's house. Then, he said, he saw them again shortly after midnight.

Hekuran Kokomani, thirty-three, is an Albanian handyman who is also believed to be a drug informant for the local police. He testified that he nearly ran into a big, black garbage bag the night of either October 31 or November 1. What Kokomani at first thought was a bag, he said, turned out to be Amanda, Raffaele, and Rudy, which caused even the jury to burst into laughter. Then, he told the court, Amanda brandished a knife at him, and in self-defense he threw his cell phones and a handful of fresh olives from the floor of his car at her.

Nara Capezzali, sixty-nine, lives in an apartment above the parking garage that overlooks via della Pergola. Her husband died in July 2007, and on November 1, she went to light a candle at his grave. That evening, she was lonely and sad. She flipped through the TV channels but didn't find anything to watch, so she took her laxative and went to bed. Around 11:00 or 11:30 P.M.—she did not look at a clock—she woke up to use the toilet. On her way back to her bedroom, she heard a scream.

"It was a woman's scream, so blood curdling it made my skin crawl," she would later testify. Then she heard what sounded to her like three or four people running up the metal steps to the top of the parking garage. She was upset all night. The next day, Capezzali saw police cars in the yard at 7 via della Pergola and heard the news of Meredith's murder.

3

"I Kicked the Door in, and Then I Heard a Scream"

NOVEMBER 2, 2007, was a frigid morning in Perugia. Fog had settled on the Umbrian hills, and the damp air was bone-chilling. Around 11 A.M., the sun started to peek through the haze, and Elisabetta Lana went out to her garden on via Sperandio to check her roses. She heard a strange ringing sound under one of the bushes and decided to call her son Alessandro. The night before, a prankster had phoned to warn that there was a bomb in her toilet, and the elderly Signora Lana was quick to worry. Alessandro called the postal police, who came by Elisabetta's just before noon. The two mobile phones they found under the roses were easily traceable. One had a foreign SIM card purchased in Leeds, England. The other belonged to

Filomena Romanelli at number 7 via della Pergola nearby.

At 12:35 P.M. the postal police pulled into the yard at 7 via della Pergola looking for Filomena. Instead, they found Amanda Knox and Raffaele Sollecito standing outside the house. Raffaele was wearing a jacket; Amanda was not. A mop and bucket stood propped against the tiny porch at the front of the house, and Amanda told the police that she was taking these to Raffaele's apartment to clean up a leak under his kitchen sink. The police, accustomed to dealing with foreign students and their imperfect command of Italian, were sympathetic to Amanda. With no idea that they had stumbled onto a serious crime scene, the police were at first not particularly puzzled to find the pair standing in the yard, looking bleary and slightly ill at ease. Later, they would testify that the couple acted "startled and nervous."

Raffaele immediately told the police that something seemed to be wrong in the house. Amanda had seen blood in the bathroom and later found a broken window in Filomena's room, so they suspected a burglary. When the police asked if he had dialed the emergency number, 112, Raffaele said yes, although phone records would later show that this was a lie—instead, he had called his sister, a police officer in Puglia. If Raf had in fact called 112, the switchboard would certainly have forwarded the call to the Carabinieri (military police) and the investigation into Meredith's murder might have gone very differently under the auspices of their crime scene unit, the RIS (Reparti Investigazioni Scientifiche). Instead, the postal police called the Polizia (state police), who called in their own crime scene experts, known as the ERT (Esperti Ricerca Tracce). The RIS and ERT are fierce competitors. The more sophisticated RIS tends to investigate Italy's most violent crimes and Mafia hits. The ERT generally handles domestic violence cases, but is eager to prove that it is every bit as good as the RIS.

While they waited for the state police to show up, Amanda called her Italian roommate Filomena and urged her to get home quickly. Raffaele made a late call to 112 in which he described the suspected break-in in whispered tones—that tape would later be played at trial. But by then, the state police were already on their way to via della Pergola. And the state police were far more constrained than the Carabinieri in what they could do without a warrant. They were also quick to trust Amanda and Raffaele and allowed them to lead investigators through the house. Carabinieri officials later said they would have made them wait outside.

Amanda told police that she had returned home from Raf's apartment at midmorning and noticed blood in the bathroom, where she proceeded to shower. Raffaele showed police the broken window in Filomena's room and explained that they had tried to open Meredith's door, but it was locked from the inside. By then, Filomena had returned home with another friend, Paola Grande, along with their boyfriends. With Meredith missing and her two phones now on the kitchen table, Paola's boyfriend, Luca Altieri, argued that they should not wait for a warrant. The police suggested that because they were on private property, the young men could break down Meredith's door without repercussions.

"With the police, we decided to break into the room," Luca later testified. The police stood back, and Filomena and the others huddled behind him as Luca attacked the door. "I kicked the door in, and then I heard a scream. At that moment I saw a pool of blood with streaks coming away from it."

The scream was from Filomena, who had caught a glimpse of Meredith's bare left foot. Amanda and Raffaele were also in the kitchen when the door came down; they were the first to run out of the house when the group in front turned and bolted, screaming, from the kitchen. But from their position at the back of the crowd, there was no way that Amanda or Raffaele could have seen Meredith's position inside the room. A few hours later, though, Amanda told the police and onlookers who had gathered outside the house that Meredith had been found in front of her closet.

That was not the case. Police investigators would later determine—according to the trajectory of blood when her throat was cut—that Meredith had been in front of the closet on her knees when she was stabbed. But then her body was dragged a few meters to the side of the bed, her long hair leaving on the floor a swirl of blood that is clearly visible in the crime scene video. That's where she died of asphyxiation, literally suffocating on her own blood. A pile of Perugia postcards that Meredith had written to friends sat on her night-stand next to a paperback book and a glass of water. The bra that had been sliced from her body was crumpled at her feet. But most notable to detectives was that someone had covered Meredith with her duvet after the blood on her body dried. The only bloodstains on the duvet came from her neck wound, not from the small drops that had splattered over her torso when she was stabbed. Criminologists agree overwhelmingly that covering the body is almost always the mark of a woman, especially if it is done after the murder. That simple detail and the fact that Amanda described Meredith's body in front of the closet, where she was murdered—not by her bed, where she was found—would stick in the mind of the prosecutors throughout the investigation.

At 1:30 P.M., Italo Carmignani, a longtime journalist for the *Messaggero* newspaper in Perugia, received a cryptic text message from a trustworthy source close to the police: *"Ragazza morta via della Pergola, forse omicidio*—Dead girl via della Pergola, might be murder." It was the first of hundreds of leaks to various journalists eager to understand this complicated crime. ERT experts arrived from Rome that afternoon, and two videographers and a still photographer documented their painstaking collection of evidence throughout the house. On the soundtrack to the video, investigators can be heard discussing the evidence and swapping hypotheses about the crime. Patrizia Stefanoni, a biologist with the ERT, personally collected many of the samples she would later test in her pristine lab in Rome. Dressed in a white jumpsuit, she picked up

Meredith's bloodied bra from the floor by the tiny elastic band between the cups.

"This was cut right off her body," Stefanoni said, shaking her head. "Imagine. And look, we're missing a piece of the bra clasp."

The police collected the lacy black underwear that was rolled up at Meredith's feet and checked the button and zipper of her blue jeans, but failed to find any evidence that these had been forcibly stripped off her body. They then lifted the comforter to look at Meredith's slender body, nude except for the blood-soaked long-sleeved white T-shirt that was pushed up over her small breasts. Her skin was purple and red with bruises, and her chest showed the outline in small droplets of blood where her bra had been. Meredith's right leg was bent slightly, and her left leg was straight. She had recently had a Brazilian—her pubic hair completely waxed. There were more bruises on her hips, knees, and thighs. But her face was still beautiful, her lips slightly parted in a Mona Lisa smile.

An examination of her vagina revealed a hair that the police removed and put into a plastic bag. "It's blonde," Stefanoni said, directing the collection officer to note that the hair was not Meredith's. Police also noted the evidence of recent sexual contact, both vaginal and anal, but no blood or internal tears that would suggest rape—thus the theory of a sex game was formed. Multiple autopsies would later fail to prove sexual assault, while at least one autopsy suggested that the sexual assault took place postmortem.

On a pillow that had been shoved under Meredith's hips, police found both a bloody shoe print and two spots that might have been dried semen. Testing for one would compromise the other, Stefanoni believed, so she would later have to decide which was potentially more important to the case. Concluding that the droplets seemed old and were probably those of Meredith's new lover, Giacomo, Stefanoni decided to focus on the bloody footprint. In the end, she could not link the footprint to anyone beyond a reasonable doubt, because it was indistinct, smudged at both heel and toe. All she could establish with certainty was that the shoe's size was smaller than that of any male suspects in the case and approximately the same size Amanda wore.

Meredith's left arm was bent, and her blood-smeared hand was still suspended in the air near her face. The tip of her long, thin index finger was soaked in blood as if she had touched her neck. But Meredith's right hand showed not even a drop of blood except from tiny cuts on the palm of her hand—it had not been near her face or neck when she was stabbed, but the detectives determined that she had extended it in self defense. The twin bruises and identical pressure points on the insides of her elbows were consistent with her arms being held back.

"It's blonde," the scientific police officer said as he pulled a long hair from Meredith's blood-soaked hand.

"She has long fingernails, doesn't she?" asked Stefanoni, examining Meredith's hand.

"She has medium long fingernails," corrected the officer. He found no skin cells under the nails to show that she struggled for her life, but he put plastic bags over both hands to preserve the nails for further analysis. The police then lifted Meredith's head to measure the knife wound in her neck.

"*Mamma mia,*" said Stefanoni.

"*E abbastanza profondo*—It's pretty deep," said the officer.

"Look, there are more wounds," said Stefanoni as her assistant moved Meredith's head. "Another cut on the other side of her neck. There must have been two knives."

"*Penso di si*—it's very likely," said her assistant.

The police rolled Meredith's body to its side and photographed and measured the many cuts and scrapes on her back. The top sheet from her single bed was crumpled in a ball near her body, soaked in blood. Investigators then used tiny metal scissors to cut out the bloodstained sections of Meredith's fitted bottom sheet still on her bed. One section showed a handprint. The other was the perfect outline of a knife.

By the wardrobe, where Meredith was killed, the police identified marks on the floor from her knees. Above where her body had been, high on the wall, were three long, bloody fingerprints, as if someone had stumbled while trying to get up. Those prints were unidentifiable, though the defense would link them to Rudy Guede; another set inside the wardrobe door— where it looked as if someone had braced for leverage while moving Meredith's body—were also too smeared to read. Although most of the fingerprints and DNA in the room would later be matched to Rudy, there were fourteen fingerprints and DNA traces that could not be identified, because they were too smeared or degraded.

After Meredith's body was wrapped in plastic and placed in a gray metal coffin to be taken to the medical examiner, the videographer swept the room again, this time focusing on the area under her bed, noting suitcases and a Zara shopping bag. He zoomed in on a black desk lamp that witnesses would later say did not belong in Meredith's room. Why had the killers moved the lamp to the floor of her room? Police then identified the white clasp of Meredith's bra but somehow failed to place it in a plastic bag. Eventually, testing revealed Raffaele's DNA on the tiny metal hook of the fastener. But it would be six weeks before investigators finally collected the clasp—ample time for the defense to argue that it had been mishandled and contaminated.

The police might have done well to stop videotaping at this point, because as they proceeded to other rooms in the apartment, they made mistakes that would hobble the prosecution and hand the defense some potentially valuable loopholes on appeal. Stefanoni and her colleagues, increasingly agitated, began to make a series of grave errors on camera. When one of her colleagues collected bloodstains from the porcelain bidet in the bathroom that Amanda and Meredith shared, she failed to change cotton swabs before collecting additional samples. In another video segment that the defense team would become fond of showing in court, it appears from the position of Stefanoni's tennis bracelet that she failed to change her surgical gloves between one contact with evidence and the next. Publicly, the prosecutors lauded Stefanoni's work on the case. But in private, they were more critical and confided to a small group of reporters that these lapses undermined what should have been an open-and-shut case.

Another mistake involved the bloody footprint from a sneaker found near Meredith's body. A few days later, it would be falsely attributed to Raffaele after police asked him to remove his shoes during an interrogation to measure them against the print. A match in size and brand became the basis on which Raf was taken into custody. But investigators failed to notice the telltale pattern left by a tiny piece of glass wedged in the bottom of the shoe at the murder scene, which would later allow the print to be positively attributed to Guede. Except for that oversight, the police would never have been able to detain Raffaele while they built a case for filing charges against him, even though he and Amanda provided conflicting alibis. In Italy, flawed alibis don't weigh as much as hard forensic evidence, and the police needed that shoe to remand Raf without a judge's order.

When they began examining other parts of the house, police found reason to believe that someone had tampered with the scene. The evidence of a break-in in Filomena's bedroom was particularly suspicious. A rock had been thrown through the window, apparently to gain entry, and the room was ransacked, with clothes pulled from the wardrobe and scattered on the floor. But the broken glass lay on top of the clothes, not under them, which suggested that the window was broken after the room was tossed. Police were also puzzled by the lack of bloody footprints leading out of Meredith's room. Whoever killed her had to have been covered with blood, yet there were only a few faint sneaker prints outside the room and one partial bloody footprint on the bath mat in the girls' bathroom, but no footprints leading up to it. Also, the rest of the house was oddly devoid of fingerprints.

After Meredith's body was removed and all the obvious forensic evidence was collected, the investigators began to spray the apartment with Luminol, a chemical that can uncover blood even after the blood has been wiped clean. Sure enough, there were a woman's bare footprints, Amanda's size, outside Meredith's room. These prints would be positively matched to Amanda, but in a serious procedural oversight, they were never tested to show conclusively that they were made in Meredith's blood. Luminol also reacts to

certain acidic substances, so without additional testing, these prints—of someone who lived in the
house—could not be directly linked to the murder.
The Luminol also revealed more blood in the bathroom and a stray drop in Filomena's room, where the
break-in occurred. That drop would prove the most incriminating; it had Amanda's DNA mixed with Meredith's blood. At the time, however, police made no
connection between the evidence of a clean-up in the
house and the mop propped against the front porch.
Several days later, when Raffaele was arrested, police
searched his apartment and found a receipt for Ace
brand bleach, purchased the morning of November 4,
2007, at 8:15. That bleach was probably used to clean
his shoes and maybe even the knife. The clerk at a different store would later testify that he saw Amanda in
the cleaning supplies section shortly after he opened
on November 2, 2007, at 7:45 A.M.

While the scientific police collected crucial forensic
evidence inside the house, the media were gathering
equally damaging circumstantial evidence from the
rooftop of the nearby parking garage. That's where the
growing number of reporters from Rome and London
joined the local press in setting up cameras aimed at
the tiny villa below. They saw the police, dressed in

white jumpsuits, comb the garden area and move quickly into and out of the house, taking bags of evidence to the waiting van. At the end of the garden, a group of young people were huddled on the gravel—friends of Meredith and of her Italian roommates. At the other end of the driveway, Amanda and Raffaele stood alone. They seemed only interested in themselves. Amanda was crumpled. Her hair was messy, and she was wearing wrinkled, faded jeans. She eventually put on an ill-fitting military jacket from Raffaele's car. Raffaele was composed—his long hair perfectly combed and his clothes fresh, a yellow woolen scarf wrapped elegantly around his neck. Raf was distracted, looking around the garden and up to the roof of the parking garage, lost in thought. He had the same look of aloof detachment that he would later display in the courtroom. As Raf followed every movement of the police into and out of the house, Amanda hugged and kissed him constantly, almost desperately, and whispered in his ear. The video and still shots of them cuddling in the cold would become Exhibit A in the court of public opinion.

Carmignani, who knew all the cops by name, broke away from the gaggle on the roof and sauntered down to the crime scene. The police confided to him some observations that never got to court. For example, police said Amanda's body odor contradicted her claim that she'd just showered; she smelled like sex. They noticed that her face was puffy, with makeup smeared under her eyes. Because she was not then a suspect, no drug or alcohol tests were ordered. Before the police sealed the crime scene, Amanda was even allowed to go back into the house unescorted to collect a few things.

That afternoon, in London, Meredith's father John Kercher heard that a British student had been stabbed to death in Perugia, and he had an immediate, gut feeling that it was Meredith. A freelance journalist for the British tabloids, John has the air of an academic, with his black turtlenecks, dark corduroy jackets, long gray hair, and sculptured beard. He would later write an article in the *Daily Mirror* describing that terrible day. The piece was published in tandem with his court testimony in Perugia, effectively scooping his colleagues on what he would tell the judge.

"Meredith's mother Arline called to say she's heard reports that a British girl student has been murdered in Perugia," John said. "Obviously there was concern, but there are thousands of British students in Perugia and you try to use that as a calming influence."

Still, John was worried, so he tried to call Meredith. His stomach dropped when he reached an automated message that her phone was off.

"For the next half hour I try at least a dozen times before it suddenly starts ringing." Still no answer. He starts to panic. "By now my instincts have kicked in. I have to get information fast."

John called the foreign desk of the *Daily Mirror* and asked what they had heard. They told him to call back in an hour and they might have more. When he called back, his editor confirmed his worst fears.

"I shall never forget her words: 'The name going around Italy is Meredith.'"

John then drove to Arline's house, where he was joined by their other children: Stephanie, John, and Lyle. "We're all distraught," he wrote in the *Daily Mirror* article. "By now, Arline has spoken to the Foreign Office who confirms the worst. At 9 p.m., Meredith's photo comes on the news. The room falls silent. We all hug."

4

"Everyone Cried Except Amanda and Raffaele"

ON NOVEMBER 3, Meredith Kercher's murder was the only thing on anyone's mind in Perugia. The coffee bars were buzzing, radio and television news carried nonstop coverage, and a steady stream of cars crept past via della Pergola to get a glimpse of the *casa degli orrori*—"house of horrors." The universities were still closed for the long holiday weekend, but the administration issued an official e-mail warning students to keep their eyes and ears open—an assassin was on the loose. The ERT scientific experts, up from Rome, had worked through the night collecting evidence and documenting the crime scene. It was still dark when an ambulance arrived to take Meredith's body to the coroner. In London, her family members were finalizing their travel plans to Italy. Meanwhile, Rudy Guede remained in Perugia, nervously milling around the city center, wracked with guilt and paranoia. Everywhere he turned, people were expressing shock and disbelief about the murder. Later, during his appeal testimony in November 2009, he told the court that he remembered it all—the blood, Meredith's scream—and he knew he had to get out of town. But he waited a whole day to do it.

Amanda woke up in Raffaele's bed on the corso Garibaldi, about a ten-minute walk from via della Pergola, around 11 A.M. They had breakfast, had sex, and then, around midday, went out to the newsstand by the basketball courts and scanned the headlines. At 5 P.M., Meredith's friends began gathering in Piazza IV Novembre on the steps of the *duomo* for a memorial. A giant color poster of her smiling face had been erected, and red votive candles glowed on the church steps, lighting the late afternoon sky. Amanda and Raffaele did not go to the vigil. Instead, they waited until it was over before visiting a boutique near the *duomo* to buy underwear for Amanda. Her apartment had been secured as a crime scene, and except for the few things she was able to grab on the way out, she had only the clothes on her back. But instead of somberly going in to buy the items she needed, she is shown on closed-circuit TV footage kissing Raffaele and laughing with him as they hold up various G-strings. In one still shot taken from the footage, Raffaele is standing behind Amanda with his hands on her hips and his groin pressed into her. A few days after their arrest, the store owner, Carlo Maria Scotto di Rinaldi, remembered their odd behavior and turned over the tape. "They came into the shop at about 7 pm and were there for about 20 minutes," he later testified in court. "She bought a camisole and G-string. I heard her tell him that 'Afterwards I'm going to take you home and put this on so we can have wild sex together.'"

On the night of November 3, Rudy went out with his friends. They drank, got high, and danced. They flirted with the students, as they always did. He could block Meredith out of his mind as long as he kept busy, but the moment he closed his eyes, he saw red. He couldn't sleep. He wandered around Perugia all night, and in the morning he packed his rucksack and got on a local train to Milan, where he would switch for the Eurostar to Austria and then to Germany. He had very little money in his pocket, but he had to get out of Perugia before someone realized that the fingerprints in Meredith's bedroom were his.

Over the next few days, Amanda was preoccupied with finding a new place to live. Her mother's cousin, Dorothy Craft Najir, urged Amanda to come to her house in Hamburg until things settled down. Amanda refused. Later, the court would hear that she wanted to stay and help the investigators. In fact, she could not have left Perugia without raising an alarm. Detectives were watching her every move. Instead, Amanda repeatedly called Filomena and Laura to ask if they could live together again and to inquire after a refund for the rent and deposit she had paid. The two Italian roommates were perplexed by her behavior, as was Meredith's new boyfriend, Giacomo Silenzi, who had been out of town when Meredith was murdered. The police were questioning all of Meredith's friends, calling them to the station in groups to iron out certain elements of the crime. On November 2, Amanda was already at the police station when Giacomo arrived by train from his parents' house in the Marche. "I couldn't help thinking how cool and calm Amanda was," he told the *Daily Mail.* "Meredith's other English friends were devastated and I was upset, but Amanda was as cool as anything and completely emotionless. Her eyes didn't seem to show any sadness, and I remember wondering if she could have been involved."

Giacomo then talked with Meredith's British friends, who all agreed that Amanda was oddly detached from this violent murder. One by one, they told the police that Amanda's behavior was suspicious. In fact, Meredith's friend Amy Frost was deeply offended by Amanda's conduct when they were together at the police station on the day of the murder, waiting to be questioned. "Amanda put her feet up on Raffaele's legs and made faces at him," she later told the court. "Everyone cried except Amanda and Raffaele. They were kissing each other." Another of Meredith's friends, Natalie Hayward, remarked to the small group of grieving friends at the station that she hoped Meredith hadn't suffered much, to which Amanda replied, "What do you fucking think? She fucking bled to death."

Amanda also told both Amy and Meredith's friend Robyn Butterworth that she had seen Meredith's body inside the closet and covered with her duvet. Amanda "kept talking about how she had found Meredith," Robyn recalled. "She sounded proud that she had been the first to find her." Robyn soon quit speaking to Amanda. Meredith's friends validated what the police were already thinking. They had also been observing the young American's curious behavior. She was, to them, so detached from the situation around her that they wondered, at times, if she was perhaps psychologically disturbed or in shock from the murder. They decided to tap her and Raffaele's phones and heard Amanda say on November 4, just three days after the murder, "I can't take it anymore."

On November 4, Amanda was called back to the police station. They were hungry, so eventually Amanda sent Raffaele out for pizza, which they ate at the station while they waited to be questioned. The police, now suspicious of the pair, had set up a surveillance camera and taped their conversation in the waiting room.

"What are you thinking?" Raffaele asked Amanda, who looked concerned.

"I don't want to be here. I want all of this to be over," she said.

Then she started talking to Raffaele about a man without naming him. "I want to know who his friends are because he doesn't have very many friends. He didn't leave the house much. He didn't talk much."

The police were convinced that Amanda was talking about the killer. They were sure that she was protecting someone.

On November 5, the police decided to call Raffaele in for questioning one more time. They had a lot of information that didn't make sense. Phone records showed that Amanda and Raffaele had turned off their cell phones at 8:30 P.M. November 1. According to the records, it was the first time Amanda had ever turned off her phone for the night. The same records showed that they then turned the phones on again the next morning just after 6, although they had told police they slept until midmorning. The police didn't want to tip them off, so neither Amanda nor Raffaele had been asked about the phones yet.

Raffaele, the police felt, was the weaker of the two; if he knew anything, they thought they might get it out of him first. Raffaele arrived at the police station at 10:40 P.M. Amanda had not been called in for questioning, but she did not have any other friends in Perugia and she did not feel comfortable staying at Raffaele's alone, so she came along. She brought her homework and sat in the waiting room studying while Raffaele was questioned. The chairs were stiff and uncomfortable. At one point, she got up to stretch her back. She did a back bend and then she bent forward and did a cartwheel and splits. Two of the police officers on duty told

Amanda to stop. They told her that it wasn't the right behavior for the situation.

While Amanda was performing gymnastics in the waiting room, Raffaele was destroying her alibi in a tiny room down the hall. His version of events of November 1 jibed with hers for most of the day; they slept in after a late night on Halloween, then spent the afternoon at via della Pergola, napping, smoking joints, playing the guitar in Amanda's room. Then they went for a walk around town for a couple of hours and split up near the basketball courts so that Amanda could go to work at Le Chic. Later, they would change their story to say that they had both stopped by Raffaele's house before Amanda left to go to work. But at the police station, he told a different story.

"I went home on my own. Amanda said she was going to Le Chic because she wanted to see some friends. That's when we said good-bye. I went home, smoked a joint and had dinner but I can't remember what I ate." He also couldn't remember Amanda being around, although she had told police, days earlier, that when Patrick Lumumba sent her a text message telling her not to come to work, she went straight over to Raffaele's and spent the entire evening there. In Raffaele's version, he was home alone around 11 P.M. when his father called on the mobile phone, as he did every night. But the police already knew from phone logs that neither this call, nor one his father made at 8:40 P.M. to the land line, had been answered.

"I remember that Amanda hadn't come back yet. I surfed the net for another two hours after *babbo* called and only stopped when Amanda got back, at about 1 A.M."

Raffaele didn't offer up any of the details that Amanda had given police about their evening—that they had watched *Amélie*, made dinner, smoked a few joints, and had sex. That was the break the police were looking for. Raffaele had not corroborated Amanda's alibi. And Amanda had not corroborated his. One or both were lying. The police asked Raffaele to remove his shoes, which they checked against a bloody footprint found in Meredith's bedroom. The print appeared to match and, unbeknownst to Amanda, who was still in the waiting room, Raffaele was arrested and taken into custody.

BY NOW IT WAS AFTER 1 A.M., but with Raffaele sitting in a jail cell, Monica Napoleoni decided there was no time to waste in bringing Amanda back for questioning.

Detective Napoleoni, forty-six, the head of the Perugia homicide squad, would make the perfect sex-flick dominatrix. She is a thin woman with long, jet-black hair that she wears in a sharp fringe just above her eyes, perfectly framing her oval face. Her perma-tan décolletage and heavy eye makeup are familiar sites in Perugia. In the winter, she tucks her tight blue jeans into black stiletto boots. During the summer, she wears white jeans, baby-doll blouses, and sandals, her toenails painted the same crimson red as her manicured nails. As her officers were booking Raffaele, Napoleoni went out to the vending machine in the hallway, worried that Amanda might hear Raffaele protesting his arrest and decide to leave.

"Who on earth could have killed her?" Napoleoni asked Amanda, her arms crossed as she leaned against the vending machine.

Amanda said that she didn't know—that she had wracked her brain and come up with nothing. The two went back to an interrogation room, where Napoleoni and several other officers asked Amanda to check through her cell phone for names and ideas. Because Amanda was not then an official suspect or person of interest, her questioning was not taped. At 1:45 A.M., Napoleoni called in a translator and wrote in her police log that Amanda was also being questioned. At that point, she was an official suspect in Napoleoni's eyes and the police should have started taping the interrogation and allowed Amanda to call a lawyer, but they didn't. The interrogators asked Amanda to read the names and text messages on her phone. When she got to the message that she had written to Patrick Lumumba on November 1, she was asked to explain what it meant. She had written in Italian: *"Ci vediamo più tardi. Buona serata."* In English, the phrase *ci vediamo* means "see you later" and is nothing more than a friendly "see you around." But in Italian, the same phrase generally suggests a fixed appointment. The interrogators would not let it go; they pressed Amanda to explain when she met Patrick and what they did together.

Amanda says that the police yelled at her and called her "a stupid liar." She says they hit her on the back of the head twice and told her that she was protecting someone. Amanda says they threatened her with thirty years in jail and told her she would never see her family again. So, she says, she came up with a story. She told the interrogators that, yes, she had met Patrick that night at the basketball courts. She said that the two of them went back to via della Pergola to find

Meredith because Patrick liked her and wanted to start something with her.

"Patrick and Meredith were in Meredith's bedroom while I must have stayed in the kitchen," she told the interrogators, who at 3:30 A.M. called prosecutor Giuliano Mignini, fifty-seven. Amanda repeated her story to him. "I can't remember how long they were together in the bedroom, but the only thing I can say is that at a certain point I heard Meredith screaming. I was scared and put my hands over my ears. I can't remember anything else. I'm so confused."

As Amanda described the scene once more, Mignini took notes. Later he was told that she had cried and hit her head over and over again the first time she told the story. Despite what would be reported later, Mignini was only in the room for the last ninety minutes of the four-hour interrogation. He did not conduct the questioning and was not the one who browbeat her into confessing her presence at the crime scene. During the time Mignini was present, he says, Amanda admitted to being drunk and passing out. He says she covered her ears when she described the screams. Then she said, "This has upset me, and I'm very frightened of Patrick." Mignini says he was sympathetic to Amanda at that moment. It made sense to him that she was afraid of her boss and might be protecting him. The police immediately went out to arrest Lumumba, who was awake, preparing a bottle for his young son; they marched him out of the house as his son and his Polish wife looked on. Amanda also told the investigators that she did not remember if Raffaele was there that night, but she says she remembered waking up at his place the next day with no idea of how she had gotten there.

Detective Napoleoni agrees with Amanda about what was said that night, but she denies the police ever hit her. She says that while the interrogation was tough, there was no physical contact. When Amanda took the stand in June, the young woman repeated the accusation that she was hit. When the judge asked her to identify who hit her, she looked around the room and said she didn't know, even though Napoleoni and all the officers present at her questioning were in the courtroom. Amanda maintains that the police badgered her until she confessed. The officers say they were firm but polite, and even offered her chamomile tea and sweets from the vending machine. Amanda and her parents would later be sued for slander for accusing the police of brutality.

Amanda's lawyers maintain that the police either destroyed the tape of this questioning or seriously erred in not making one. Mignini says that investigators don't usually tape interrogations of witnesses unless they are sure they are going to get something. And, because Amanda had not been officially called in as a suspect, the room they took her to wasn't equipped for such surveillance. But if the interrogation had been taped and played in court, it could have hurt both sides. If police were heard cuffing her, they could be charged with assault. But if the jury had heard Amanda describe being in the house and hearing terrible screams, it would have been even harder to believe her later story—that she had spent the entire evening at Raf's.

AT 5:45 A.M. on November 6, Amanda signed a written statement, in Italian, and was arrested. Because she did not have a lawyer present, that statement was never admissible in the criminal case against her. But it was used in the civil case filed by Patrick Lumumba for defamation—a case that ran in tandem with the criminal trial. His lawyers translated it back into English:

> Raffaele and I had smoked a hashish cigarette and so I
> felt confused, as I neither use drugs nor heavy drugs

frequently. I met Patrick just afterwards, at the basket place of Piazza Grimana and I went home with him. I do not remember if Meredith was there or if she came after. I have trouble remembering those moments but Patrick made sex with Meredith, with whom he was infatuated, but I can't remember well if Meredith had been threatened first. I remember confusedly he killed her.

Patrick sat in jail for two weeks while the police tried hard to find evidence against him. The only thing they could come up with was the presence of his cell phone in the area around via della Pergola the night of the murder. But that ping was later determined to be a technical anomaly. As the police eliminated evidence against Patrick, however, they became ever-more sure that another person was involved in the crime. The fingerprints in Meredith's room did not belong to Patrick, Amanda, or Raffaele. They ran a crosscheck and quickly matched them to Rudy Guede, who, like all immigrants in Italy, had been digitally fingerprinted as part of his legal alien residency status. After a further DNA match was made to Rudy, he was found and arrested in Germany, and Patrick was released from prison. The day's headline read simply: "One Black for Another."

AMANDA'S MOTHER, Edda Mellas, arrived in town November 6, the day of her daughter's arrest. Edda had already made plans to come, at Amanda's request, to help her resettle after the murder. By the time she arrived, Amanda was in prison, and Edda found herself scrambling to put together a legal team and battling the reporters who had gathered outside Capanne prison. It would be her first taste of the media circus, and she proved to be a producer's dream; she slammed the car door and wept in plain view of the camera. The court had already assigned Amanda a local attorney, Luciano Ghirga, a grandfatherly man who was well known and respected in Perugia. A former soccer star and communist politician, Ghirga is friends with all the judges and prosecutors in town, which is certainly an advantage, but he doesn't speak English. So Edda also asked the U.S. Embassy for recommendations and selected Carlo Dalla Vedova from its alphabetical list. Dalla Vedova is a well-known civil lawyer in Rome, whose clients include some of the big multinational firms and U.N. agencies, but he had never tried a criminal case.

Before the attorneys had a chance to meet each other or their new client, Amanda asked her prison guards for paper and a pen. Then she wrote a five-page memorandum that would seal her fate by essentially confirming the statements in her late-night interrogation:

> I also know that the fact that I can't fully recall the events that I claim took place at Raffaele's home during the time that Meredith was murdered is incriminating. And I stand by my statements that I made last night about events that could have taken place in my home with Patrick, but I want to make very clear that these events seem more unreal to me [than] what I said before, that I stayed at Raffaele's house.
>
> I'm very confused at this time. My head is full of contrasting ideas and I know I can be frustrating to work with for this reason. But I also want to tell the truth as best I can. Everything I have said in regards to my involvement in Meredith's death, even though it is contrasting, are the best truth that I have been able to think.

In this spontaneous statement, Amanda placed herself at the scene of the crime, and she was never able to convincingly remove herself in further testimony. Amanda had always been a prolific writer, and she continued this habit in prison, rambling on, incoherently at times, in what she called "My Prison Diary—*Il mio diario del prigione.*" The police took every page and used it against her, painting a picture of a disturbed, sometimes delusional young woman. Among other things, Amanda wrote:

I only know I'm safe when I'm with the police or alone, although this is only the kind of safety I feel for my body. Alone, and with the police, I fear my mind. Alone I imagine the horrors my friend must have gone through in her final moments. My imaginations become more and more precise the more the police ask me questions. For instance, I know my friend was raped before she was murdered. I can only imagine how she must have felt at these moments, scared, hurt, violated. But even more I have to imagine what it must have felt like when she felt the blood flowing out of her. What must have she thought? About her mom? Regret?

By November 7, Meredith's parents had also arrived in Perugia, and they visited the makeshift shrine on the steps of the *duomo*, where the giant picture of their daughter still stood among the red votive candles. John placed a red rose in front of the picture and wrote a note on a piece of paper he had in his pocket: "Love you forever Meredith. All my love, Dad XXXX."

Meredith's parents were not allowed to take their daughter home on this trip. Two further autopsies were ordered, and it would be six weeks before her body was released and laid to rest at the Croydon Parish Church in South London in a service attended by hundreds. A wreath of yellow chrysanthemums on her casket spelled out "Mez," as she was known to her friends. Amanda's family never offered any condolences to Meredith's parents, who struggled to understand what had happened to their daughter. As headlines screamed the morbid details of her murder, Meredith's parents became reclusive, refusing to talk to any press. Only Meredith's sister Stephanie gave sporadic interviews, describing their faith in the Italian justice system. The Kerchers' lawyers, Francesco Maresca and Serena Perna, drip-fed the worst details to the family in the most delicate way they could. The only thing Meredith's family requested was that the nude photos of her battered body not be released to the press. It would take nearly two years to get any sort of answers about what had happened to Meredith that night, and even then, the day after the verdict, they still did not know exactly how or why she had been killed. Three people had been convicted, yet her murder remained a mystery.

5

"The Worst Part Was I Still Couldn't Remember Exactly What I Had Been Doing"

FROM THE MOMENT they were arrested, Amanda Knox and Raffaele Sollecito were a circulation bonanza for the Italian media and a front-page staple of the British tabloids. The Italian press funneled leaks from the lawyers and prosecutors to embellish the crime story and quickly dubbed Knox "Angel Face," fostering a cult of morbid fascination with this most unlikely killer. The tabloids in the United Kingdom, eager to defend the honor of a British victim, mined the saucy details Amanda had inadvertently provided on the Internet, beginning with her MySpace screen name:

"Foxy Knoxy." Calls to teachers and friends in Seattle routinely produced descriptions of an all-American kid, studious, smart, and athletic. But the social networking sites told a somewhat different story. A YouTube video of Amanda drunk spawned the image of a party girl, although, in truth, nearly every coed in America has posted a similar clip. But other entries suggested a darker, more enigmatic personality. "Baby Brother," a short story Amanda posted on MySpace, is not too unsettling overall, but it includes a rather cavalier reference to rape:

> Kyle laughed deep in his throat. "Icky Vicky, huh? Jeez, Edgar. You had me going there." He picked up his calculus book and flicked with his thumb to find his page, shook his head side to side with his smile still confident on his face. "A thing you have to know about chicks is that they don't know what they want." Kyle winked his eye. "You have to show it to them. Trust me. In any case," He cocked his eyebrows up and one side of his mouth rose into a grin. "I think we both know hard A is hardly a drug."

("Hard A" is Seattle slang for hard alcohol and usually refers to a toxic cocktail of vodka, whiskey, and schnapps. Amanda and her friends often partied with pot and hard A rather than beer for maximum inebriation.)

Whether or not Amanda meant to condone sexual violence, prosecutors took this story as proof that she had at least fantasized about it. It was there in her mind. Add drugs and alcohol, they reasoned, and it wouldn't take long for such hidden thoughts to lead to action. And other MySpace entries, including this one, titled "The Model," posted a few weeks before the murder, seemed to compound this picture of a young woman with a vivid, vaguely lurid imagination:

Small, cold fingers curled around my open hand and I gasped, ripping my hand away. Aislin, narrowed hazel eyes and immobile pink lips, flipped on the light of the stairway and stared at me. She was quiet, and the hand that had reached for mine hung limp in the space between us like the wrist was broken. I grabbed her hand back and held it to my lips, kissing the little fingers. It drew her closer to me and she pulled weakly for her hand back. "What are you doing?" I didn't let her go, but grabbed her wrist and pulled her toward the front window. "Did you lock the back door when you came home from school?" I searched the dark space in

front of our lot. "You're late, again." Her voice was
earthy and slightly bitter, like red wine.

A picture was forming of Amanda as a vixen with
dark impulses, and her family struggled to control the
firestorm. They insisted that "Foxy Knoxy" was a nickname Amanda earned for her junior soccer moves, not
her sexual magnetism. Time and again, they denied
that she ever used the moniker as an adult, despite the
fact that it was her MySpace ID. (Among the thirty-
nine social networking friends on her stepfather Chris
Mellas's MySpace page was "Foxy Knoxy," which
linked to Amanda's page.) The image wars proceeded
with thrusts and parries: On morning TV shows, Edda
would weep and show pictures of Amanda kicking a
soccer ball; in the afternoon, the British tabloids
would trumpet headlines about her jailhouse lesbian
encounters (drawing inferences from entries in her
prison diaries and letters to friends, where Amanda
worried about becoming gay). Meanwhile, all sorts of
people tried to make a buck off the murder. Amanda's
classmates in both Perugia and Seattle asked for cash
or plane tickets in exchange for interviews. One of her
teachers in Italy offered a TV producer a handwritten
letter of Amanda's—for 10,000 euros. Tidbits from the

legal dossier were shopped around. Coverage of the crime began to diverge on the two sides of the Atlantic. From the vantage point of Perugia, it seemed as though the Knox family's American supporters were simply choosing to ignore the facts that were coming to light in Italy.

Raffaele had also supplied some troubling information on his social networking sites. He was a rich kid with ready cash to fund a drug habit, and in one Web entry, he bragged about spending "80 percent of his waking hours high." The background image on his Web pages was a marijuana leaf print, and in almost every picture, he appeared bleary-eyed and tousled. (A police wiretap later heard his father say, "Raffaele, I've told you, *basta spinelli!* —Enough with the joints!" The most damaging picture he posted would be forever etched in the minds of anyone following this case: Wrapped in surgical bandages, Raffaele brandishes a meat cleaver and a jug of *alcool,* a pink, alcohol-based cleaning liquid.

These were the scraps of information that stoked a media frenzy in Italy. Even before Amanda and Raffaele were officially charged with murder, they were on the front page of every newspaper in the country, usually under headlines such as "*Amanda, Sangue e*

Sorrisi—Amanda, blood and smiles" and *"Uomini e Segreti, Amanda Racconta*—Men and secrets, Amanda tells all." As Amanda's and Raffaele's popularity grew, so did the hunger for information about them. Amanda's face graced the cover of Italy's most popular grocery aisle glossies, and the murder was the subject of four quick books by Italian journalists. One of the books even came with an animation of the alleged crime on DVD.

THE AMERICAN PRESS HUNG BACK, at first objective and somewhat disbelieving that such a wholesome-seeming girl could have any connection to such a sordid foreign crime, and then, as the family stepped up its defense, increasingly divided between two camps that would become simply the *innocentisti*—those who believed she was blameless—and the *colpevolisti*—those who did not. In Perugia, these labels governed access. The prosecutors and defense lawyers all thought they knew exactly where each journalist stood, and those of us who were deemed American *colpevolisti* were few and far between. Of the handful of American journalists in Perugia in late 2007 and early 2008, none got access to the Knox family without certain guarantees about positive coverage. Within months, the family decided to speak on the record primarily to the American TV networks, often in exchange for airfare and hotel bills. Most of the print press was shut out. And the TV producers learned to be very cautious about being seen with people like me, lest the Knox family should cut them off.

As interest in the case grew, an odd assortment of American talking heads attached their reputations to Amanda's innocence. An aggressive support group called Friends of Amanda formed in Seattle, headed by Anne Bremner, a media-savvy criminal lawyer who had cut her teeth as a tough prosecutor in Seattle's King County Court. She then became a defense lawyer, taking on some of America's most outrageous cases. (For example, she represented the Des Moines, Washington, police department when it was charged with failing to protect an underage student from sexual relations with schoolteacher Mary Kay Letourneau, who bore two of his children.) A youthful blonde, Bremner was already a network regular before anyone ever heard of Amanda Knox. The attorney had provided round-the-clock media commentary on the Michael Jackson pedophile case and the Scott Peterson murder trial. Bremner quickly embraced Amanda's cause pro bono, even though the family claimed they'd never met her. Bremner honestly believed that Amanda was being railroaded in Perugia, but she also wanted a piece of the media attention whirling around the case. She frequently spoke on the family's behalf and might have served them well as the official spokesperson. But the family had other ideas. They hired David Marriott, a mustachioed ex-journalist-cum-public-relations-guru who specialized in crisis management for some of Seattle's troubled politicos.

Very quickly, Marriott lost control of the situation. As he spoon-fed the Knox-approved message to American outlets that couldn't afford to send correspondents to Italy, those of us on the ground in Perugia began passing his contradictory e-mails around as entertainment during the long days in the court. In one instance, Marriott confirmed to me that ABC News had paid for Amanda's parents to fly to Perugia in exchange for exclusivity. When I confronted my friend Ann Wise, an ABC producer based in Italy, she quickly passed on the leak. ABC got a denial from him that he had ever told me this—despite the fact that I had an e-mail to prove it. Similarly, in the spring of 2008, he told me that the Knoxes would not give interviews, and then Rachel Donadio of the *New York*

Times had a sit-down with Amanda's father, Curt Knox. Marriott told me that Rachel must have doorstepped Curt in Perugia; she confirmed that Marriott had set up the interview for her. What Marriott failed to realize was that the Italy-based press corps was a close-knit group that could not be played against each other.

Meanwhile, the networks started vying for the Knoxes' attention with their own legal analysts. Among the first was Joe Tacopina, a sexy Italian American New York lawyer who keeps a media clip file of his high-profile cases. His famous clients included Jordan Van der Sloot, the Dutch student implicated in the murder of Natalee Holloway in Aruba, and Raffaello Follieri, Anne Hathaway's rogue Italian con man. In the spring of 2008, Tacopina came to Perugia as a paid consultant for ABC News to investigate the real story behind the Kercher murder, and I interviewed him for *Newsweek* in Rome in March. He said he was acting as a consultant to the family, even though he was being paid by ABC, and he was the first to call foul on the missteps by Italian investigators. But he also told me that deep down, he wasn't sure about Amanda's story.

"Her best defense, I think, is probably going to be the truth. Am I saying she didn't make mistakes? No.

And do I know for a fact that she's innocent? Of course not."

That was the end of Joe Tacopina's involvement in the case and the beginning of more aggressive message control out of Seattle. Andrea Vogt, a Bologna-based freelancer stringing for the *Seattle Press-Intelligencer*, wrote her own story about Tacopina's behavior in Perugia, and Marriott quickly tried to shut her down. Typically, Marriott denied that my interview had even taken place, and he told Andrea that "the reporter got it wrong." Not convinced, Andrea called me. I gave her a transcript of the interview and a copy of the tape, and we began what would be a two-year battle against the Seattle message machine, incurring personal attacks and outright threats. Andrea and I became known on the pro-Amanda blogs as "Void and No Clue," and I was often referred to as a "failed travel writer," despite a career of thirteen-plus years covering Italy's major news events for *Newsweek*.

THE PUSH-BACK FROM SEATTLE was ferocious, but the message discipline was imperfect. When Bremner told CNN that Amanda needed the U.S. State Department to rescue her, Marriott would simply quip, "Anne doesn't speak for the family" or "I don't keep up with what Anne is doing." Moreover, Amanda's Seattle supporters began to compromise the work of her legal team in Perugia. On August 12, 2008, Seattle judge Michael Heavey wrote a letter titled "Request to transfer the trial against Amanda Knox out of Perugia," using Superior Court of the State of Washington letterhead. The headlines in Italy incorrectly interpreted this as "American Judge Wants Trial Transferred to America," which infuriated Knox's local counsel. By the time Heavey retracted his letter a few months later, with an apology to the Italian Justice department, the damage had been done. The Perugia judge who denied Amanda's request for house arrest said that one of the reasons was flight risk and that "the American judge who would have to sign her extradition back to Italy" would not cooperate. Knox's attorney, Luciano Ghirga, told reporters outside the courthouse in Perugia, "The American lawyers do not represent anyone here."

Meanwhile, the blogosphere began to crackle with acrimonious exchanges between those who believed that Amanda was innocent and those who did not. The first blog dedicated to the crime, Perugia Shock, was set up on November 2, 2007, the day Meredith's body was discovered. The blogger, Frank Sfarzo, a skeletal man with a waxed crew cut, ran a student flophouse in town and believes that he missed a call from Meredith while she was looking for lodging. When I later asked him in an e-mail why he started the blog, he explained the missed connection and described how Meredith had looked at the coroner's: "Seriously, she was so beautiful and sweet, she seemed to be alive, with her eyes open, with the mascara on her eylashes [sic], just like ready to go out."

Sfarzo hid behind the handle "Frank the blogger," and he would never confirm whether he actually saw Meredith on the autopsy table or simply saw the coroner's photos. He ingratiated himself with several clerks and cops around town and, curiously, often had a document no one else could get or a scoop that beat out the rest of the press. He started out as an objective observer, slightly sympathetic to Meredith, but became a rabid proponent of Amanda's innocence. He was the quintessential blogger—a smart, cryptic insomniac. Even the chief prosecutor, Giuliano Mignini, read his posts.

MIGNINI ALWAYS BELIEVED that Frank's blog was intellectually inspired and financially subsidized by Mario

Spezi, the Italian journalist who covered the Monster of Florence serial killer for *La Nazione*. During the 1970s and 1980s, several couples were murdered as they made love in their cars in the foothills around Florence. Spezi followed the investigation for years and pinned his reputation on a theory of the case that Mignini disputed. Eventually, Mignini had Spezi jailed for obstruction of justice and tampering with evidence.

Enter best-selling author Douglas Preston, who went to Florence in 1999 to follow a dream and write a thriller based in the fifteenth century and centered on a lost painting by Masaccio. He stumbled into the Monster of Florence case when he discovered that one of the murders had occurred near the villa he had rented for the summer. He soon met Spezi, and the two forged an intense friendship and working relationship that produced the best-selling book *Monster of Florence*. That nonfiction book makes Spezi's case that the Monster was part of a conspiracy that started in Sardinia. Mignini maintains that the killer was Francesco Narducci, a local doctor with strange sexual tendencies. Because Narducci's body was found floating in Lake Trasimeno near Perugia in 1985, the investigation into his death was under Mignini's jurisdiction, which allowed the prosecutor to reopen the moribund Monster of Florence case. In doing so, he says, he offended prominent Florentine judges who didn't want the small-time Perugian prosecutor nosing around.

Mignini believed that Spezi and Preston were concerned that the Narducci theory might undercut their story line or imperil their movie deal with Tom Cruise, and he suspected they might go to extraordinary lengths to promote their version of the crime. So, as is often the case in Italy, Mignini ordered a wiretap on Spezi's phone. (He also wiretapped several other journalists and police officials, for which he would later be convicted of abusing his office.) Andrea Vogt and I listened to those wiretapped conversations between Spezi and Preston on a hot summer day sitting in Mignini's office in Perugia, and, as he alleges, they do seem to refer to steering the police to faked evidence. On the basis of those tapes, Spezi was arrested and sent to prison for a month. Preston was also called in to see Mignini.

"He didn't understand anything," says Mignini, who believes that Preston was duped by Spezi. Mignini describes this conversation in gentle terms. He says Preston was nervous and did not understand Italian.

Mignini told him that perhaps he needed a lawyer, but denies ever asking him to leave the country. But Preston tells a very different story. He says Mignini browbeat him for two hours, accusing him of a crime he did not commit and threatening him with jail. Preston was terrified to the point of having to excuse himself to use the toilet during the interrogation. After Amanda Knox was arrested, Preston quickly stepped forward to corroborate her claim of being abusively interrogated, recounting his own experience with Mignini to an American press eager to embrace the narrative of a corrupt, rogue prosecutor "railroading" an innocent American—even though Mignini was barely present at Amanda's interrogation.

MIGNINI LOOKS LIKE a balding teddy bear and favors shabby chic cotton trousers and a faded jacket. I have spent hours and hours with him, in his office and in more casual settings. I also sat in the Florentine courtroom where he was being tried for abuse of power, which became part of the brief against him in the Knox coverage. The main charge in the abuse case was that Mignini and a former Florentine policeman-turned-crime-writer ordered a forensic analysis on the state's budget rather than the police budget—which did not necessarily affect the outcome of the testing, but did anger the powerful Florentine judges who thought the Perugian prosecutor was trying to interfere with a local investigation. On January 22, 2010, Mignini was acquitted of the primary charge of improperly ordering up the forensic analysis, but convicted of abuse of office for lesser charges, namely, wiretapping journalists and other police officials close to the case. He was given a sixteen-month prison sentence, but in Italy sentences of less than two years are not required to be served, and at the judge's discretion, Mignini's sentence was suspended. Prosecutors in Italy are often accused of corruption, and in the Italian legal system, even the most banal charges must be investigated, which clogs the court dockets with relatively inconsequential cases. Moreover, these minor convictions are rarely grounds for stripping a prosecutor of his or her responsibilities.

None of the charges against Mignini were directly related to the Knox case, nor were they that unusual; wiretapping journalists is a national pastime in Italy, and most of us assume we are frequently intercepted. But the fact that Mignini was being prosecuted for misconduct—even if it happened more than ten years ago — was a great boon to the Friends of Amanda. The Knox camp issued press releases depicting him as a judicial rogue and exaggerated the gravity of the charges against him. They also used the fact that Mignini was on trial for wiretapping journalists as a veiled threat to anyone who might try to cultivate the prosecutor as a source. His conviction, however, posed a new dilemma: How could Knox's supporters argue that the Italian justice system was hopelessly corrupt when it appeared to work just fine against Mignini?

Mignini is not the evil figure described by Preston. Nor is he the deeply religious, humble truth seeker he claims to be. He is somewhere in the middle. He is not prone to mistakes and wild theories, as Preston contends. But he is not beyond them, either. Among other things, he is quick to suspect Satanism in some of the more grisly crimes he investigates. In the early days of his involvement in the Monster of Florence case, Mignini called in a Roman sorceress named Gabriella Carlizzi to advise him personally on Satanic signs and symbols. But he subsequently fell out with Carlizzi, a familiar figure around Rome and Perugia who channels her dead priest, and even had her arrested on a number of occasions. When Mignini first heard of the ghoulish paraphernalia in the house on via della

Pergola, he was not thinking about Halloween, but instead thought he had stumbled on another Satanic rite. But that theory never made it past the preliminary hearings, though Mignini tried to reintroduce it in the closing arguments.

At the same time that the Knox family was painting Mignini as a vindictive lunatic, it was flooding the Web with pictures of "honor student" Amanda playing soccer and holding babies. Unfortunately, those images were undermined by Amanda's behavior in Capanne prison outside Perugia. In the weeks after her arrest, she wrote a diary that would provide even more fodder for the hungry press. Certain favorable pages of the diary were leaked by Amanda's defense lawyers, but that simply tipped reporters to its existence, and the entire thing was part of the official 10,000-page case dossier—the holy grail that every journalist wanted on his or her hard drive. Documents became the trading currency in covering the Knox case, and they were used as bargaining chips by the prosecutor, lawyers, and journalists.

WITHOUT QUESTION, Amanda's prison writings—illustrated by stick figures with smiley faces, castles, and evergreen trees—were disturbing. She obsessed about the murder, writing about what Meredith's final moments must have been like and searching her foggy memory:

> I lay quietly on my bed, thinking, crying, sleeping. I wasn't hungry and when they told me to eat I got a stomach ache. And the worst part was, I still couldn't remember exactly what I had been doing at my boyfriend's apartment. This was my great mystery that I had to answer, and I couldn't. And I knew if I couldn't remember this it would be reason enough for the police to think to accuse me, which I learned later was exactly what they were doing.

At times, Amanda seemed to revel in her new notoriety and at one point even wrote about her fan mail:

> I received 23 fan letters today that I think the guards have been saving up for me from at least the past couple of days. That makes the count up to 35 letters. Oh yeah, and I got a postcard from the post office saying I have a package too. Fun . . .
> As for the letters themselves, they vary, and are all from guys ranging from 20-35 on average . . . Some ask

me to have faith in God. Others bash the Italian justice system. The majority comment on how beautiful I am. I've received blatant love letters from people who love me from first sight, a marriage proposal, and others wanting to get to know "the girl with the angel face" . . . I think the same thing about this as I did before. If I were ugly, would they be writing me wishing me encouragement? I don't think so.

She was less certain about where she stood with Raf:

Something interesting that has come up is about Raffaele. Apparently he told newspapers (though who can trust them) that all I've done is made his life crazy and he wants nothing more to do with me. Ouch.

Raffaele also wrote a diary as he waited for the trial to begin, complaining, as befits his privileged upbringing, about having no slippers and no one to clean the toilet. He described the cold floors in his cell and the Moroccan inmates next door who beat their heads against the wall screaming for another dose of heroin. During the summer of 2008, Sollecito began writing to his hometown paper, effectively developing his own column, which always began *"Cari Amici della Piazza*—dear friends in the square," a familiar political cry in Italian villages. "I continue to serve my sentence in hell before being convicted of a crime," he informed the folks back home in Puglia. "I hope someone will remember that I'm still here and that I'm innocent." He supplied vivid details about living in isolation and befriending a family of cockroaches.

Every scrap of information about Amanda and Raffaele—every photo, every diary entry—was front-page news, avidly consumed throughout Italy and especially in and around Perugia. Most Italian trials are decided by a panel of judges, and only in rare circumstances do they include additional jurors who, in fact, are called "civilian judges." Their names are drawn from a computerized list with no vetting about their opinions or their exposure to the case, and they are compensated for their time according to their level of education and current salary. The investigation of the Kercher murder dragged on for nearly a year, and for all that time, those who would eventually be called to sit in judgment on Amanda and Raf were bombarded by sensational journalism about them.

The Italian system does, however, allow for a quicker "fast-track" trial if a defendant agrees to fewer witnesses and limited evidence. And that's what Rudy Guede, arrested November 20, 2007, fourteen days after Amanda and Raffaele, requested.

6

"I Am Not the One Who Took Her Life. But I Didn't Save Her"

RUDY GUEDE'S INVOLVEMENT in the death of Meredith Kercher, and how that relates to the prosecution of Amanda Knox and Raffaele Sollecito, has been the most misreported aspect of this case. The Knox-friendly American press usually told the story like this: Amanda, Raffaele, and Patrick Lumumba were all arrested in the early days of the investigation, and then the police found the real killer, Rudy Guede. The authorities soon released Lumumba, but in order to save face—so important in Italian culture!—they stuck with their original theory of multiple killers and refused to let the two nice white kids go free *even after Rudy was convicted of the murder!* This was the line taken, for example, in this exchange with CNN's legal analyst, Jeffrey Toobin, in June 2009:

JEFFREY TOOBIN: Well, I just think—the thing that people don't realize about this case is that someone has been convicted of killing this woman. There is the guy—

CAMPBELL BROWN: One of the guys, he's already in jail.

TOOBIN: He's already in jail and he's been convicted based on DNA evidence, and seems like pretty good evidence of killing this woman with a knife. Why is this woman on trial now?

ANCHOR JAMIE FLOYD: Well, I'll tell you why. I'll tell you why she's on trial. Because as in our country, certainly over there, the authorities went out in front of the story. They put themselves on the line, naming this young woman and her boyfriend and they don't want to admit a mistake. It's that simple. They don't want to admit they made a mistake, nor does the media.

The reality is quite different. Most importantly, Rudy was convicted as one of three killers, with the judge in his fact-track trial voicing his conviction that Rudy acted in consort with Amanda Knox and Raffaele Sollecito—in essence, laying the groundwork for their convictions. But because Rudy was appealing this ruling when Amanda's and Raffaele's trial got under way, he could not be compelled to give evidence in the trial of the two lovers, and the testimony from his original trial was not public—fast-track proceedings never are. Rudy, however, has also changed his story and left many questions unanswered about the events of that night.

Rudy was no stranger at via della Pergola. All of the guys downstairs knew him well, both as a friend and as a drug supplier. He had met Amanda and Meredith downstairs as well, and by Amanda's own admission, he had chatted with her in the center of Perugia among a group of friends. Rudy had even asked one of the guys downstairs if Amanda was dating anyone. Born in the Ivory Coast, Rudy came to Italy with his family illegally by boat when he was five years old. His father left the family when Rudy was sixteen, and the teenager spent the next several years with a wealthy Perugian family who helped him legalize his status. He studied hotel management but lost interest in school and supported himself with odd jobs, working in gardens, on local farms, and at the student bars. He lived on the periphery of the university scene in Perugia and could easily pass for a student. He was known to be a small-time drug dealer, and as a registered immigrant, he had fingerprints on file with local police. In his own instance of ill-considered social networking, he posted a YouTube video of himself as Dracula saying, "I want to suck your blood." Rudy was a good basketball player who spent most afternoons on the Piazza Grimana courts near the via della Pergola. Although when Amanda-friendly sources described Rudy as "an African man," they seemed to imply—accessing subliminal racism—that he was a big, powerful guy, the truth is that he has a slight build, with narrow shoulders and sunken eyes.

Police believed from the beginning that several people were involved in Kercher's death. They felt relatively certain that Amanda and Raffaele had some role, but also suspected that these two were covering up for a third person. Amanda was pressed on that point in her late-night interrogation when, under intense questioning, she finally fingered a different black man, Patrick Lumumba, who was quickly arrested. But a Swiss professor named Roman Mero came forward to say he had been at Patrick's bar the night of the murder, giving him an ironclad alibi, and the police eventually let the bar owner go. But for months, they tormented Patrick, auditing his books and checking his financial and residential status. In an attempt to save face—and to avoid a false imprisonment suit—the police had hoped to charge Lumumba for something, but they never could. Yet they still had evidence of a third killer: feces in the toilet did not match any known person with access to the house, fingerprints in Meredith's bedroom did not match either Amanda or Raf, and a black hair was consistent with someone of African descent but was not Patrick's.

The fingerprints produced a sure match to Rudy, then twenty-one, who had left town. Police proceeded to take DNA samples from a hairbrush at his Perugia apartment and issued an international warrant for his arrest. Within a few days, his DNA was matched to the fecal matter at the villa. And after his name was released, a number of witnesses came forward to describe Rudy's strange behavior the night of the murder, reporting that he had been at the Domus nightclub around 2:30 A.M. on November 2. No one recalled seeing blood on his clothing, but at least three people testified that he had "extremely bad" body odor.

BY THEN, Rudy was in Germany, staying in touch with some Perugia friends via the Internet. Police convinced his friend Giacomo Benedetti to start up a Skype conversation, which they monitored, and they then traced the IP address to Dusseldorf. Prompted by police, Giacomo asked Rudy about Amanda. Rudy said, "Amanda doesn't enter into this," and her supporters quickly seized on the fact that Rudy initially admitted that Amanda was not involved. But in the same conversation, he also said that he was not involved.

"Listen, you know I knew those girls, I knew them both, Meredith and Amanda, but nothing more, you know that," Rudy told Giacomo. "I've been to their house twice, the last time a few days before all this business, but I didn't do anything. I have nothing to do with this business. I wasn't there that evening. If they have found my fingerprints it means I must have left them there before."

Giacomo told Rudy that the police were looking for him. So when Rudy was stopped for fare-beating on a train between Mainz and Wiesbaden, in a panic he confessed to the train cops that he was wanted for murder in Italy.

Rudy's flight to Germany counted against him at trial. Even though Rudy was taken into custody in

Germany as a murder suspect, the authorities there did not interrogate him. But his father, Roger Guede, who hadn't seen his son in more than five years, flew to Germany and was able to visit him and give him the latest news from Italy, where rumors were swirling about Amanda and Raffaele's possible involvement in Meredith's murder. *Il Messaggero*'s Carmignani also traveled to Coblenza prison and spoke to Roger Guede after his visit. "He keeps repeating that he didn't kill her," Rudy's father said, shaking his head. "That's all he says. I'm his father, but what can I do? Nothing. I wasn't there for him before, he doesn't want me to be there now."

VALTER BISCOTTI ALSO DASHED to Germany to offer Rudy legal services, free of charge; he is always eager to insert himself into headline-making cases. A small, hunched man with closely cropped, graying hair, he constantly walks up and down Perugia's corso Vannucci in quick, short steps, drumming up business and looking for reporters. His suits are loose and his shoes are scuffed. Known as "the Jackal" to Italians and as "Cookie Man" or "Biscuit Man" to the Anglo press — a play on his last name — Biscotti has made his career defending public enemies and unlikely victims. In one of his reputation-making cases, he won a civil judgment for the family of an undercover police officer killed by Red Brigades terrorists. He is also currently representing the family of "Brenda," a Brazilian transsexual whose mysterious death is linked to an admitted affair with a prominent Roman governor. Biscotti brought Brenda's mother from the Amazon to make the TV rounds, and he is famous for selling access to his clients—reputedly charging Universal, the parent company of NBC, sixty thousand euros for a jailhouse chat with Rudy. (NBC denies making this payment. Biscotti says the interview is scheduled to take place in March 2010.)

That is roughly the amount of his fee for defending Rudy, but Biscotti took the case pro bono immediately after Guede's arrest. He frequently charges media outlets for "photocopies" of documents and "secretarial fees" related to long, on-camera interviews. Because he feared racial bias if Rudy was tried with Amanda and Raf, Biscotti requested the fast-track trial, which involved only a few witnesses in addition to the forensic evidence. At that proceeding, in October 2008, prosecutors demonstrated that most of the DNA samples from Meredith's room, including incriminating traces on her body and his bloody handprint on the pillow underneath it, belonged to Rudy. Nevertheless, the state's autopsy results showed that more than one person killed her. Luca Lalli, the coroner who first examined Meredith, would testify during Amanda and Raffaele's trial that the size, shape, and location of Meredith's dozens of cuts and bruises could only be explained by more than one assailant. She had finger bruises around her neck. She had a bruise on her chin and over her mouth, as if someone pressed a palm to her chin, covering her mouth and scratching her nose. She had identical bruises on each of her inner elbows, compatible with her arms being held back. There were also small, finger-size bruises on her body consistent with a female hand and, on her pillow, a small, bloody shoeprint that could never be positively identified beyond the range of Italian sizes 36–38. Amanda wears size 37.

Rudy was convicted of sexual assault and murder and acquitted of theft. He was sentenced to thirty years, which, because he chose the fast track, was essentially guaranteed to be reduced on appeal. Although he has steadfastly denied murdering Meredith, by the time he got to court he admitted being in the house, no doubt because the proof of that was irrefutable. In essence, Rudy changed his story three times. When he was arrested, he said simply that "some Italian guy" had done the killing; during his fast-track trial, he said that unknown assailants had beaten him up; at his appeal hearing, he said that it was Raffaele and that he heard Amanda's voice and saw her silhouette through a window. His reward for placing them both at the scene would be a substantial reduction in his sentence.

MIDWAY THROUGH the Knox trial, while Rudy sat in prison waiting on his appeal, Biscotti threw himself a fiftieth birthday party. The invitation for the April 23, 2009, event declared the theme to be "Don't Look Back in Anger"; the venue was listed simply as "The Red Zone," no address needed. This faded disco down the hill from Perugia's city center is a wildly popular spot with the university students. But it also attracts Biscotti's crowd, the generation that christened the club when it opened about twenty-five years ago, which explains the pulsating, red-neon palm trees and Heart's "Barracuda" screaming from the sound system. By choosing The Red Zone, Biscotti was making a statement about his celebrity as a player in the Knox drama. The guest list made a statement of a different kind about the small, insular world of Perugia's legal establishment.

As Biscotti, wearing a white bandana to match his bell-bottom pants, played lead guitar on a true-to-original rendition of "Smoke on the Water," Paolo Micheli, the judge who convicted Rudy of Meredith's murder, sat on a red sofa tapping his foot in time. Monica Napoleoni, head of the Perugia homicide squad, stood nearby with her sidekick Lorena Zugarani, the burly policewoman whose karate kick broke the window to the downstairs apartment in via della Pergola. (That kick, caught on video, became infamous among Amanda's Seattle supporters, who used it as an example of shoddy police work, wrongly asserting that Zugarani was breaking a window in the girls' apartment, not the one downstairs.) Various other faces from the Knox trial—legal assistants, Mignini's briefcase man, and a couple of guards—mingled in the wings. Because it had been one of those rare days when the hearing ended early, only a few members of the foreign press were still around: John Follain of the *London Sunday Times*, Chapman Bell of NBC,

Andrea Vogt of the *Seattle Post-Intelligencer,* and me. But the reporters had certainly all been invited; Biscotti made a point of knowing every journalist by first name.

"You were a little bit hard on Rudy in your last piece," he would often say to me, laughing. "I could file a defamation suit, but I won't this time." (He has lodged suits against Joe Tacopina and Doug Preston for saying publicly that Rudy is the lone killer.)

"How's Rudy doing?" I would ask frequently.

"Tranquillo," Biscotti always says. "He's studying, just like Raffaele. He's writing, just like Amanda. He will come out with an education. A degree. He is using this time to better himself."

ON NOVEMBER 18, 2009, just two days before closing arguments began in Amanda and Raffaele's trial, Rudy stood before an appeals judge and for the first time spoke publicly about the night of the murder. He said he knew Meredith; they had met in the basement apartment on via della Pergola because he was friends with the four guys who lived there. They saw each other at a Halloween party and started talking, and he says she invited him to come over the next night.

"We didn't have an appointment," he testified. "She had just said I should come over, so I just went over and she let me in."

Then, he says, the two of them started to kiss and things were moving along. But he said that neither of them had a condom, so they stopped and started talking. Rudy said that Meredith was complaining about Amanda. She checked her purse and noticed that money was missing, so she immediately blamed Amanda.

"'My money, my money,'" he recalled Meredith saying. He heard her add, "'I can't stand her anymore.'"

Then, he says, he had a stomach cramp and had to use the bathroom. Meredith told him to use the bigger one down the hall. He put on his iPod and listened to four songs, during which time he heard the doorbell ring. He said he then heard Amanda and Meredith arguing, and a few minutes later, he heard a scream. He says he quickly came out of the bathroom, not even taking time to flush the toilet. He saw a man he did not know at the time, but who he later realized was Raffaele. He said he saw Amanda's silhouette outside the window and heard Raf say to her, "Let's go, there's a black man here." Then Rudy said he went into Meredith's room to find her bleeding. He moved a pillow under her and pressed a towel on her neck to try to stop the blood. He didn't know what to do. He freaked out and ran away.

"Every time I close my eyes, I still see red," he told his appeals judge. "I am not the one who took her life. But I didn't save her. That's the only thing I can apologize for." Then Rudy turned to the Kerchers' lawyers and told them, "I want the Kercher family to know that I didn't take their baby girl away, and I didn't rape her."

Rudy's story is far-fetched. It is just too bizarre to believe that this man would have been at Meredith's house on the very night her roommate and a lover set out to murder her—and that he would have gone to the toilet at the precise moment they came in. He testified to hearing a doorbell ring, but why would Amanda ring her own doorbell? It is unlikely that Meredith and Rudy had any plan to meet. None of Meredith's friends saw him at the parties they attended the night of Halloween. Neither Rudy's nor Meredith's cell phones showed any trace of contact between the two. The more likely scenario is that Rudy met Meredith just twice. Once, in the downstairs apartment where they were all getting high, and the second time on the night she was murdered. Rudy says that he and

Meredith made out but stopped short of sex, yet Meredith's body showed signs of vaginal and anal penetration and his DNA was present on her body. As Francesco Maresca, Kercher's lawyer, told me once, even though the autopsy did not find conclusive evidence of rape, the bruises on her body were not compatible with even rough sex; they were a result of sexual assault. "Sex that ends with someone dead is not consensual," Maresca declared. "Rudy's story is unbelievable."

But it is equally far-fetched to believe, as the Knox camp argues, that Rudy acted alone to kill Meredith. Leaving aside the coroner's report, he simply wasn't strong enough to overpower her, sexually assault her, strangle her, and kill her with two different knives, leaving wounds on both sides of her neck without her fighting back—and there was no evidence of that. Rudy's presence in the murder room is undeniable, although what happened there remains unclear.

The prosecutors never believed Rudy's story beyond his admission that he was in the house when Meredith died. They have always thought that he met up with Amanda and Raffaele and that the three went to the house together to sew up a drug deal. In fact, one person at the Knox trial testified that he had seen

Amanda and Raffaele with Rudy in the days before the murder. However, this person, Albanian immigrant Hekuran Kokomani, who works odd jobs around Perugia and is rumored to be a police informer, was seriously compromised when he was arrested for cocaine possession a few weeks before he appeared in court. (A popular *colpevolisti* theory is that the drugs were planted to try to keep him quiet. The *innocentisti* disagree.)

Another witness testified that he saw Amanda and Raffaele near the house the night of the murder. Antonio Curatolo, a bearded homeless man who lives on a park bench next to the basketball courts, was wheeled into the courtroom wearing his usual stocking cap and blanket for a coat, which gave the defense ample ammunition to brand him unreliable, in light of his peculiarities. Yet his testimony was surprisingly credible. Curatolo is obviously educated; he was the most politically correct witness at the Knox trial, referring to Rudy as a "man of North African descent" instead of *il nero*—the black guy. He knew Rudy from watching him play basketball and complimented his athletic skill. Curatolo was lucid in his descriptions of the area near the crime scene and convincing when he placed Amanda and Raffaele there, testifying that the two stood at the gate and watched the house around 9:30 P.M. and again at around 10:30 P.M. on November 1.

AS GUEDE'S APPEALS JURY was deliberating on December 22, Valter Biscotti made his usual *passeggiata*, looking for reporters, but many of the foreign press had left town after the Knox verdict. He eventually ducked into the Sandri sandwich shop and saw me. He ordered his lunch and brought it to my table to predict exactly what was going to happen next and explain how he planned to defend Rudy in the third and final stage of his appeal, to the high court.

"This time, they will not absolve him," he said between bites of polenta. "Rudy has promised to cooperate even more with the investigators, so they will cut his sentence first down to twenty-four years and then by one-third." (A fast-track defendant automatically gets a one-third sentence reduction on appeal.)

"So he's going to admit they all killed her together?" I asked.

"Rudy didn't kill her, as I've told you many times," he said. "Rudy is going to tell them what Amanda said to them both that night."

"She told them to kill Meredith?"

"Directed Raffaele," he said. "She orchestrated it all."

"And he did whatever she said in exchange for what?"

"Sex," he said. "Promises and enticements. Raffaele is weak."

"And Rudy?"

"Rudy was in the bathroom; he came out and it was all over," he said, repeating Rudy's usual line. "Rudy has never changed his story."

Biscotti paid for my lunch, and then, a couple hours later, his prediction came true. Rudy's sentence was cut to sixteen years. At first, the *innocentisti* thought this might be good news; if Rudy's sentence was knocked down that much, perhaps Amanda and Raffaele would be set free on appeal. But it soon emerged that the appeals judge agreed that Rudy killed Meredith with Amanda and Raffaele—not alone. Not only had one more judge endorsed their guilty verdicts, but he may have reduced Rudy's sentence in return for helping the prosecution strengthen its case against the other two on appeal. But Rudy's lighter sentence is also more in line with those routinely meted out in Italy for manslaughter, not premeditated murder. So it may also reflect that even in the far more exhaustive trial of Knox and Sollecito, prosecutors never conclusively established a motive for the killing of Meredith Kercher. Very early in the case, investigators suggested that the murder was the product of a Satanic ritual, because of the Halloween paraphernalia found in the villa and at Raffaele's apartment. Then they theorized that a drug-fueled sex game had gone terribly wrong before settling on the hypothesis that Amanda had encouraged the assault on Meredith to punish her prudish disapproval of Amanda's lifestyle. In Mignini's eyes, Amanda's narcissistic personality fueled a growing anger, and finally her jealousy of Meredith was too much to bear. She killed Meredith in an unstoppable rage.

But the prosecutors could never make any of these scenarios entirely convincing, although they would spend eleven months trying.

7

"DNA Doesn't Fly"

"MEREDITH WAS MY FRIEND. I did not hate her," Amanda Knox tells the jury at her trial, after the prosecution finishes two days of fiery closing arguments, describing Knox as an angry young woman who was motivated by hate and fueled by drugs and who killed in a sexual frenzy. "To say that I wanted to take revenge against a person I liked is absurd," she continues, speaking in the fluent Italian she learned in prison. Then she adds, "I had no relationship with Rudy—oh, *mama mia!*—Everything that has been said in these last two days is pure fantasy, it's not true, I have to insist on this."

Amanda's insistence on her innocence comes at the end of an eleven-month trial that sometimes feels more like a TV reality show than a legal proceeding—albeit one staged amid fifteenth-century religious art. The *aula,* or courtroom, for Meredith Kercher's murder trial is two levels underground in Perugia's ancient provincial courthouse. A glorified metal ladder and another flight of steep, worn stone steps lead down to the room called the Hall of Frescoes, which has brick walls, giant arches, and incongruous fluorescent chandeliers that look like shiny halos hanging from the ceiling. In this strange netherworld, Judge Giancarlo Massei sits under a huge crucifix facing a painting of a bare-breasted Madonna suckling her child. He is a slight man with a nasal voice that he rarely raises. Instead he gestures like an orchestra conductor to impose order in the court. His nickname among the press is "Woody," for Woody Allen. He is a serious man with a gentle smile, but he is a tough judge. In the six months before the trial of Knox and Raffaele Sollecito, he has handed down three life sentences.

The trial is procedurally complex, because the criminal charges against Amanda and Raffaele are being tried simultaneously with a civil suit filed by the Kercher family and a defamation action lodged against Amanda by Patrick Lumumba. The forensic duels can be mind-numbing, as when a cell-phone network expert goes into great detail about the vagaries of phone signals in hilly Perugia to dispute evidence from Raf and Amanda's call logs. Even the prosecutor falls asleep on occasion, and one elderly juror becomes well known for napping after lunch.

Judge Massei sits in the middle of the wide wooden bench, flanked by his co-judge and six jurors in green, white, and red sashes. The red-haired, middle-aged juror on Massei's far right glares at the prosecutor and smiles at the Knox family. In the beginning, it was the other way around, but she softened when Edda Mellas testified, feeling a mother's pain. The brunette next to her appears tortured by her duty and cries sporadically; she does not want to believe that these two young people are killers. The man on her left with long, wavy gray hair looks thoughtful and kind. He is divorced and has lost a son; he knows that life is not predictable and that good people can do bad things. Beside him is Beatrice Cristiani, the second judge. She primly takes copious notes and often checks the legal tomes piled between her and Massei.

To Massei's immediate left is the jury foreman, a criminal lawyer whose office was involved in an early phase of the Kercher murder investigation. Beside him sits my favorite juror—a pretty woman with short red hair who is surely a student of body language. She listens intently to each witness, watching their hands and faces like none of the other jurors. The juror next to her is the elderly man who tends to doze off in the afternoons. The final juror is the first alternate, an ash-blonde woman whose face I will never forget. Throughout the trial, she glares at Amanda and her family with contempt.

Another person who stares at Amanda is Lumumba, attending most hearings because of his civil defamation case. A Congolese refugee, he is a kind soul who managed, against all odds, to build a successful business in Perugia—until Knox accused him of murder. Then, many who had loved him quickly nodded their heads and said, "Well, yes, of course. He is black. Of course he killed her." His club, closed while he was under investigation, soon failed because of a falloff in business, and Lumumba's lawyer, Carlo Pacelli, lit into Amanda with the self-righteous fury of a Baptist preacher when it was his turn at summation.

"Amanda is a talented and calculated liar who went deliberately out of her way to frame Patrick," he tells the judge, reminding the jury how she had told police that she "covered her ears as Patrick murdered Meredith."

Amanda stares forward as the jury turns to see her reaction. One of her lawyers, Luciano Ghirga, put his arm around her. The other, Carlo Dalla Vedova,

124

touches her hand. "It was all a lie that marked his destiny," continues Pacelli, his face turning red. "It was ruthless defamation that destroyed Patrick as a man, husband and father." As Pacelli builds up steam, his voice grows louder and louder, and Amanda slumps further in her chair.

"You've heard the stories about her hygiene, about how messy she is. Well she is unclean on the outside"—he pauses, allowing the courtroom to go silent in anticipation—"because she is dirty on the inside."

"Who is the real Amanda Knox?" he asks, pounding his fist on the table. "Is she the one we see before us here, all angelic? Or is she really a she-devil focused on sex, drugs, and alcohol, living life on the edge?"

"She is the *luciferina*—she-devil." At that point, even the judge is regarding Amanda quizzically, trying to decide whether that description could be true.

AMANDA AND RAFFAELE don't come to court through the front door, like most defendants. Their shared police van pulls up to the back of the building, and they are escorted into cells in the back dungeon, where they wait with their lawyers for court to convene. The photographers stand on chairs and jostle on ladders to get the best view of Amanda coming in. She smiles coyly and, like Princess Diana, lowers her head then lifts her eyes to look up at people. She is a pretty woman, and she knows it.

Each day, the Anglo press forms a consensus on her appearance. Is this light blue or powder blue? Do we say hooded sweatshirt or just hoodie? Who do you suppose French-braided her hair? followed by laughter and a lesbian joke. Obviously, no one on Knox's mostly male legal team thought to coach her on courtroom demeanor until the very end of the trial: Don't wear sexy clothes when you're on trial for a sex crime. Don't smile at Raffaele. Don't look so happy. On Valentine's Day, her tight pink T-shirt read "All You Need Is Love," and the Beatles reference was a particular affront to the British press, covering the murder of a British student.

Raffaele got better advice and always wears effeminate, nonthreatening hues—lime green, baby duckling yellow, bubble gum pink. He started lifting weights in the fall, and his growing muscles are obvious through his pastel shirts. Amanda and Raffaele interact with each other in the courtroom, mouthing *how-are-you's* and passing chocolates. Amanda frequently looks confused. She studies each witness and then, eyes wide, looks at the prosecutor, often as if she has never seen him before. Many times, she doodles on a yellow pad. Occasionally, she lays her head on the desk. Sometimes, Raffaele just stares at Amanda, completely fixated. By the end, he looks desperate.

LIKE MOST TRIALS IN ITALY, this one was in session only two days a week—with additional time off for holidays and a summer break. This is the true flaw in the Italian judicial system: a lack of sufficient courtrooms and judges to handle an overabundance of cases, so it is rare to have any trial run on a Monday-to-Friday schedule. In addition, Raffaele's lead lawyer, Giulia Bongiorno, is a member of parliament in Silvio Berlusconi's party, so she could not devote full time to saving Raf from prison. As a result, the hearings stretched over eleven months. The prosecution took the first five months to present its case, embellishing thin forensic evidence with circumstantial inferences and testimony meant to convey the dark character of Amanda.

Early on, a string of witnesses who became known in the press room as "the British virgins" appeared one after another in conservative, buttoned-up clothes.

They blushed when they described Amanda's vibrator and her many lovers—never mind that they had all been out partying with Meredith until 6:30 A.M. on Halloween.

"Meredith complained that she brought men back to the house," said Sophie Purton, the friend with whom Meredith had had dinner the night of the murder. "This was something we didn't do, but Amanda was quite open about her sex life."

Amy Frost had her own complaints. "Amanda would play the guitar, but sometimes she would play the same chord over and over."

All of the British friends concurred that Amanda seemed strangely unaffected by the murder in the days after Meredith's body was discovered. "I found it difficult to be with her because she showed no emotion when everyone else was really upset. We were all crying, but I didn't see Amanda cry," said Robyn Butterworth. "She and Raffaele were kissing and joking together, there was laughter at some point. I remember Amanda stuck her tongue out at Raffaele. She put her feet up on his lap and they were kissing and cuddling and talking."

In Italian court cases, defendants can make spontaneous declarations at any moment, although there is usually nothing spontaneous about it. Whenever Raf or Amanda were going to speak, their lawyers tipped the press to make sure everyone was present. You could see the defendants rehearsing beforehand, reading notes and mouthing the words. Amanda first spoke on February 13 after listening to Meredith's British friends. Breaking a silence of fifteen months since her arrest, she tried to explain the vibrator and reclaim her image.

"It was a gift, a joke," she said, laughing. Then she showed the judge how long it was—about four inches—by spreading her thumb and forefinger. She ended her three-minute interjection with "I am innocent. I have faith that the truth will come out."

Raffaele also intervened on three occasions. But each time he opened his mouth, he sounded like a spoiled rich kid. He complained that the trial was a "terrible mistake" and that he "wouldn't hurt a fly." He complained about being cold in his jail cell and about how, during the investigation, the police took his shoes and left him in stocking feet on marble floors in the November cold. Barely mentioned in the testimony about Amanda for months on end, he declared at one point that he was not her "dog on a leash." Yet minutes later, he would be staring and smiling at her across the table. Raffaele was the odd character at the trial, at times looking more like a pimply teenager than a twenty-four-year-old university graduate accused of a sex crime. His moment of glory came when Prosecutor Manuela Comodi's computer froze as she tried to show a video of the crime scene. Raf, who had just completed his computer technology degree in prison, got up and expertly fixed the problem, his every move broadcast on the giant monitor in the courtroom.

THE PROSECUTION'S strongest forensic witness was Patrizia Stefanoni, the pretty, dark-haired specialist from Rome who collected most of the key pieces of evidence from the crime scene and then personally tested them in her lab. She was on the stand for two days and proved unflappable despite the fact that much of what she was presenting was open to challenge.

The most solid evidence came first. Five spots of mixed DNA and blood were found around the house.

Because the girls lived together, it was not so surprising to find their DNA mixed. But in the bathroom the girls shared, there was a spot of Amanda's blood mixed with Meredith's blood on the tap, on the edge of the sink and again on the side of a cotton-swab box and the drain of the bidet. The most damning spot was in

Filomena Romanelli's room, where there had been an attempt to suggest a break-in. There, investigators again found a spot of Meredith's blood mixed with Amanda's DNA. As Stefanoni noted, the spots on the sink and in Filomena's room were found only after the application of Luminol, which can reveal stains that have been wiped clean.

"Isn't it logical that two people who share a house would have mixed DNA in the house?" asked Amanda's lead lawyer, Carlo Dalla Vedova, on cross-examination.

"Not in the context of a homicide," replied Stefanoni, later adding, "although we may never know exactly what happened that night, the DNA evidence points to the fact that both Knox and Sollecito were there."

The alleged murder weapon, a twelve-inch kitchen knife found in Raf's apartment, proved to be the most contested exhibit in the case. It only matched one of the three wounds on Meredith's neck and did not match the bloody knife print left on her bed sheet, suggesting that a second knife had been used in the crime. Also, the knife was mishandled on its way to Stefanoni's lab, transferred from a plastic bag to a box. Stefanoni testified that the knife had tiny scratches on the side "consistent with scrubbing" and said that she had found traces of bleach on it. At the top of the handle, she detected Amanda's DNA profile, as if it had been left by a thumbprint. She also found seven traces of human biological matter—flesh, not blood— between the grooves at the tip of the blade. But the samples were small, and there was only enough to run one test. She notified the defense's forensic experts, who were invited to join her in the lab in accordance with the protocol for criminal investigations in Italy. They all declined, saying they felt sure there would be no match and traveling to the lab in Rome would be a waste of their time.

"But your experts had the opportunity to be there, as was their right," Judge Massei scolded the lawyers for Amanda and Raffaele. "They chose not to go, they were given ample notice."

So Stefanoni tested the blade sample alone in her lab. Her notes indicated that her initial finding was, as she wrote in English on the report, "too low." But then she amplified the settings of her equipment to the very limit of Italian and international forensic guidelines. Only then did she find a match to Meredith's DNA. Because she had no material left to double-test, that result should have been thrown out—no forensic protocol allows for single-tested evidence. But the prose-cutors took it anyway and built their case around it. On cross-examination, the defense had a heyday.

After getting Stefanoni to admit that she had written "too low" at least four times on her report, Bongiorno, Raffaele's lead lawyer, turned to the crime scene video that documented the collection of evidence and pointed out Stefanoni's diamond tennis bracelet on the outside of her surgical gloves.

"Is that your beautiful bracelet?" asked Bongiorno.

"Yes," said Stefanoni slowly.

Bongiorno then watched the video as Stefanoni moves to another sample. Her diamond bracelet is in the same location outside the glove.

"Look! Look! There it is. You didn't change gloves at all, did you?" Bongiorno gloated. "Did these mistakes happen in your lab, too?"

Stefanoni admitted her mistakes, but insisted that her results were still valid. "If the blood evidence is a positive match, it is not always important how much there is. A match is a match, and the material on the blade matches the victim."

Throughout the trial, Giuliano Mignini, the lead prosecutor, was described by the Seattle-fed U.S. press as a hot-tempered monster who had abused author

Douglas Preston years earlier and was inclined to wild theories. But it was his co-prosecutor, Manuela Comodi, who proved the real hothead. The dark-haired, beautiful woman clinging aggressively to her youth wore tight Max Mara pantsuits and designer sneakers under her black court robe and sported dangling bracelets and a giant diamond ring that added a touch of sparkle to the courtroom. When she heard the defense's Dalla Vedova questioning his paid consultant Sara Gino about Stefanoni's mistakes at the crime scene and again in the laboratory, she slammed her fists on the table and stormed out of the courtroom, returning a few minutes later with an elaborate black lace fan to cool herself.

"Pardon me, your honor, but it is hard to keep calm when the defense is insulting the state's forensic expert," she said, smiling. "They are calling her a liar. I could easily say the same about them, but it's not professional." A chain smoker, Comodi often finished her questioning with a cigarette in one hand and her lighter in the other, barely waiting to get out to the hall before lighting up. Mignini left all the technical questioning to her because she was adept at tripping up witnesses and winning back any ground lost on cross-examination.

Comodi loved props. Once, in order to prove a point about footprints, she removed her own shoe and walked around in her stocking feet to show the jury how the sole of one shoe could not be easily confused with the sole of another. During her closing arguments, she pulled a bra out of her handbag and wrapped it around her microphone stand, using a letter opener to simulate how she believed Raffaele removed the bra from Meredith's body.

She also had a playful sense of humor. She asked Michele Battistelli, one of the first police officers on the scene, about his shoe size to refute defense claims that the size 11 prints at the villa could have been made by the investigators. A big man, he answered, "Size 13," at which Comodi giggled and blurted out, *"Complimenti!"* (alluding to the old saw that shoe size correlates with penis size).

Many of the prosecution's witnesses were called simply to refute charges of sloppy police procedures. Alberto Intini, head of the Rome forensic unit that collected the evidence, was challenged by Dalla Vedova about the presence of Raffaele's DNA on Meredith's bra clasp, collected weeks after the crime. Finally, frustrated by his unit's being portrayed as keystone cops, Intini declared, "DNA doesn't fly!"

THE MOST HEARTBREAKING WITNESS was Meredith's sixty-three-year-old mother, Arline Kercher, who looked out at the audience to describe her daughter's death. "It's not just the death, but the nature of it, the violence," she said. "It's such a shock to send your child to school and for them to not come back. We will never, never get over it." Meredith's family filed a civil suit against whoever was found guilty of killing their daughter, which accomplished two things: It prevented any guilty parties from profiting from the crime through books or movies, and—because the civil suit was heard in tandem with the criminal charges—it allowed them to have their own lawyers in the courtroom, who could present witnesses and cross-examine anyone who took the stand. The Kercher's lead lawyer was Francesco Maresca, a fit, sexy, suave Neapolitan with long brown, wavy hair and blue eyes. His suspenders, his stylish fitted suits, and the tiny handcuff key chain hanging out of his back pocket were the focus of much female attention in the press corps. His father was a famous police official in Florence, involved in many high-level investigations, including the Monster of Florence, and Maresca spent a lot of his childhood under protective police escort. Sitting at the glass table in his Florentine office one evening, he told me that he does not generally take on civil cases. He mostly represents Mafia clients and hard-core criminals. "I'm used to having clients put their pistol on the table before they sit down," he said.

Part of Maresca's brief was to prevent the media from molesting the memory of Meredith. At his request, images of her body were only shown in closed-doors sessions with reporters relegated to the upstairs pressroom, where the tiny television monitor was fixed on the lawyers and jury. Several of the jury members looked away at the most gruesome parts. Amanda would not look at all; she either doodled on her notebook or turned her chair away from the monitor. Raffaele stared at the screen, at times seeming mesmerized by the images in front of him.

It is not automatic in Italy that the civil lawyers for the victim agree with the prosecution's theories, but in this case they did, and whenever Mignini's team faltered, Kercher's lawyer Maresca picked up the slack. To bolster the defense's case, for example, Dalla Vedova called a witness to knock down the idea that the signs of a break-in had been staged. Retired police marshal Francesco Pasquali produced a PowerPoint presentation trying to prove how it was possible for someone of Rudy Guede's height, weight, and athletic prowess to toss a nine-pound rock at a window thirteen feet above the ground, break the glass without also breaking the narrow wooden frame, then scale the brick wall and open the window through the small hole in the glass without leaving any traces of fabric or blood.

Maresca, who understood how important it was for the prosecution to prove that the alleged break-in was staged, started slowly.

"So your special training as a physicist or engineer makes you an expert at rock-throwing dynamics?" he asked slyly.

"No, I am a ballistics specialist," Pasquali replied.

"Have you ever conducted rock-throwing experiments before?" Maresca inquired. "Why don't we get to see the raw video of the actual experiment instead of this edited version? How many times did it take you to hit the window?"

"No, this was the only one I've ever done," he stammered, clearly shaken. "It took more than a couple tries."

"Did you try the experiment with shutters closed, like they were the night of the murder?"

"No," Pasquali admitted.

"Did you throw the rock overhand or underhand?" Maresca continued.

"Overhand."

"Why? Is that the logical way to throw a nine-pound rock up to a thirteen-foot-high window? Such an impact would have shattered the window, there would be glass outside on the ground, too. Why was there glass on top of the clothing? Can you answer any of those questions?"

"I have no idea," Pasquali said before slinking off the stand.

NO ONE IN THE JURY spoke English, so the defense tried to limit the number of witnesses who required a translator, understanding that translation would dampen the effect of their testimony. Edda Mellas was the only member of Amanda's family to take the stand. She did not want to testify, but the defense thought she would be helpful because she received a telephone call from Amanda in the early morning hours of November 2, 2007. Alas for the defense, Edda was too honest, and her testimony didn't help her daughter. She told Mignini during questioning that, yes, she had received a call from Amanda on the morning of November 2, 2007—three calls, in fact, the first one around 4 A.M. Seattle time. Since daylight savings had not kicked in yet in the United States, that meant the call was made at noon in Perugia—well over an hour before police found Meredith's body. The prosecutors always felt that Amanda made that call to her mother in a panic or to set in place an alibi of some sort. After all, people who live overseas, even for a few months, quickly learn to know what time it is back home. As a rule, Amanda would phone home at 3 or 4 P.M. in Perugia, just when her mother was getting up to go to work. So calling when it was the middle of the night in Seattle was a red flag and became an inconsistency in Amanda's story that lodged in the minds of the jurors.

"She said, 'I know it's early' but she called because she felt someone had been in her house," Edda testified through a translator. "She called again, twice more. The second phone call was that people were yelling and they found a foot in the room. She was very upset. It was disturbing. I said, 'Oh my God.' She couldn't understand, only the foot." Edda was referring to Meredith's bare foot, which the roommates had seen sticking out from under her duvet.

But this testimony contradicted her daughter's statement on the stand just a week earlier. Back then, Amanda had testified that she did not remember making that first call to her mother.

In fact, there was a lot that Amanda couldn't remember when she testified at the tail end of the prosecution's case. This was the most-attended court date of the entire trial, save the verdict, and Amanda arrived with a large cold sore on her upper lip, yet she did not look particularly nervous. She was clearly ready to speak her mind. Her low alto voice was smooth and calm, but she was not sympathetic. She came across as arrogant, at times interrupting Mignini so that she could finish a random thought. She started her testimony in English, but quickly became frustrated by the stop-and-start cadence of her translator. After two hours, she switched to fluent Italian marked by a strong American accent. But she did little to explain why she had falsely accused Lumumba of murder and even less to establish a solid alibi. (As soon as she got a lawyer, Amanda had reverted to her original claim that she spent the entire evening at Raf's house—not at via della Pergola, hearing Meredith scream.)

Amanda simply brushed off questions that she thought were below her. And when Comodi aggressively pressed her about the phone calls to her mother, she was belligerent.

"During the conversation you had with her in prison, even your mother was amazed that you called her at midday, which is three or four o'clock in the morning, to tell her that nothing happened," said Comodi.

"I don't know what had happened," stammered Amanda. "I just called my mother to say we had been told to leave the house and that I had heard something."

Comodi pressed on: "But at midday nothing had happened yet, the door had not been broken down yet."

Amanda was cocky. "OK. I don't remember that phone call. I remember that I called her to tell her what we had heard about a foot. Maybe I did call before, but I don't remember."

"You did do it," whispered Comodi, smiling. A hush fell over the courtroom.

"Ok, fine, I did then," said Amanda sarcastically. "But I don't remember."

Like so many moments during the trial, the tension in the courtroom began to rise. Amanda's lawyers were fidgeting, and Mignini leaned back in his chair. At that point, Judge Massei interrupted the testimony to bring order back to his courtroom. He softly patted the air with outstretched hands to calm things down. "*Scusata, scusata, per favore, per favore* — excuse me, excuse me, please, please," he said, smiling gently. Then he turned a serious face to Amanda.

"You don't remember, but the prosecutor just pointed out to you a phone call that your mother received in the night. So, it must have been true. It happened. Did you usually call her at that time? Did it happen on other occasions? At midday in Italy? At that time in Seattle? People don't usually call each other in the middle of the night."

Amanda nodded. "Yes, yes, of course."

"So either you had a particular motive, or it was a habit," said the judge.

Amanda's two days on the stand heralded the beginning of the defense's case. Her appearance did little to dispel the image that had been put forward by the prosecution of a disturbed young woman who might be capable of heinous acts. The defense had a lot of work to do.

8

"She Is Not Amanda the Ripper, She Is the Amélie of Seattle"

WHEN THE PROSECUTION RESTED its case, the lawyers for Amanda Knox and Raffaele Sollecito had a choice to make. They could either work at cross-purposes, each group to save its own client, or the lawyers could stay united and risk a joint conviction. Thanks to his father's money and powerful connections, Raffaele had the more experienced defense team. His lead lawyer, Giulia Bongiorno, was easily the most powerful person in the courtroom, and Amanda's attorneys never waivered from their strategy to ride her coattails.

Bongiorno is a small, birdlike woman who pecks at her sandwich and takes quick sips of her coffee during the lunch breaks. Her head darts back and forth as she speaks, and her eyes seem to look everywhere at once. But she is a powerhouse. A prominent member of parliament for the Italian prime minister Silvio Berlusconi's own party, she is a household name in Italy—a sort of Italian Johnnie Cochran often involved in the flashiest legal cases. She made her reputation defending former Prime Minister Giulio Andreotti on Mafia charges when she was in her twenties. The prospect of losing this high-profile case was not something she took lightly.

During the preliminary hearings, Bongiorno had clearly wanted to defend Raffaele without carrying Amanda as extra baggage. Amanda noted in her prison diary on November 23, 2007: "I'm waiting on Raffaele also apparentely,[sic] because he's my alibi. His lawyers, however, are convinced that I'm evil and want to have him express this. However, Raffaele apparently has been trying to tell the truth."

Bongiorno physically distanced herself from Knox's lawyers at early press conferences and often backhanded Amanda, telling reporters that the evidence against Raffaele was minute in comparison with that against Amanda and Rudy. Raffaele's father, too, rued the day his son met Amanda and told reporters privately that he thought Raffaele should have a separate trial. After all, the only forensic evidence linking Raffaele to the crime was proving easy to discount. The knife from his apartment was already discredited before the trial began because of the single testing of the DNA. More troublesome was Raffaele's DNA on the clasp of Meredith's bloody bra. But the clasp had been kicked around her room for six weeks, so this match could be challenged, too. Moreover, Bongiorno surely knew that an Italian jury would have been more sympathetic to her client if he severed ties with Amanda—she could present him as the sexual naïf who was bewitched by this American siren and did whatever she told him—even lie. Because, of course, one of the biggest pitfalls for the defense was that Raf and Amanda had contradictory alibis. That is essentially why, although Raf gave several spontaneous statements, he never took the stand to face cross-examination.

But Bongiorno is a strategist, not a risk taker. She also knew that if she turned against Amanda, the scene could get very ugly very quickly, starting with revelations about Raffaele's serious drug problems and his strange obsession with knives. Plus, no matter how tainted it might be, his DNA was in the room where the murder took place; Amanda's was not. In the end, Bongiorno knew that in order to save Raffaele, she had to also save Amanda—something Amanda's lawyers were not exactly accomplishing on their own.

And so Bongiorno used her closing arguments on Raf's behalf to give Amanda one of the biggest boosts of the trial, describing the pretty American as a simple young woman who could not possibly have masterminded such an attack. Referring back to the French art film *Amélie* that the two suspects supposedly watched at Raf's apartment the night of the murder, Bongiorno described Amanda as extravagant and unusual. "She is a little bizarre and naïve," Bongiorno told the court. "But she is not Amanda the ripper, she is the Amélie of Seattle." It could have been a turning point in the trial—suddenly, someone other than her family was sticking up for Amanda. But it came too late.

Amanda's own lawyers were less effective. Carlo Dalla Vedova, brought in by the family from Rome because he was fluent in English, had never tried a criminal case. His law practice serves Rome's power brokers—the United Nations, the Saudis, various business entities—and he is often spotted in hotel lobbies along the via Veneto closing deals. Amanda's other attorney was Luciano Ghirga, a former soccer star gone soft. Ghirga's white hair and provincial charm make him lovable. He is the typical country lawyer who knows the deepest secrets about everyone in Perugia. Ghirga had experience with criminal cases, and he knew that the most skeptical journalists were the ones he needed to court. The Knox family had the opposite view and directed him never to speak to the *colpe-volisti* reporters. But he brushed off the Knoxes with a shrug of the shoulder and bought us more wine and dinners than all the other lawyers combined. He was a charmer, with a formidable crush on Andrea Vogt, which we leveraged for inside details about the case. At times, Ghirga and Dalla Vedova weren't even on speaking terms, and more than once, I walked into the Turreno café to find them in a heated debate. If Ghirga—a Perugia insider—had been the lead lawyer, the case may have gone differently. But he was sidelined by the flashier Dalla Vedova, whom the family trusted infinitely more, if only because they could actually speak with him. Yet at times it became apparent that Dalla Vedova exploited the language barrier to shield Amanda's parents from troubling evidence.

"Carlo says there is no mixed blood evidence," Edda once told me over a beer at the Joyce Pub.

"But there is," I told her, explaining the five spots and where they were found.

"Carlo says that's wrong, and that they won't be accepted by the court," she said, clinging to every false hope he had given her.

Dalla Vedova was easily the most attractive lawyer in court—a tall, muscular tennis player with white spiked hair and playful eyes. But he was the butt of many jokes in the press room. His unorthodox tactics and bizarre questions during cross-examination often generated howls of laughter after hours, and even Ghirga rolled his eyes when asked about the star attorney from Rome. Dalla Vedova missed the final day of closing arguments for Amanda and moved on to a big-money deal with the Saudis while the jury was still out. He came back just in time for the verdict.

The unsung hero of Amanda's defense team was Maria del Grosso, a striking young lawyer who took over from Dalla Vedova during the final rebuttal arguments. She gave the most heartfelt defense of the entire trial, and the jury clung to every word. The only woman on Amanda's defense team, she was authoritative, especially when she talked about the theory that the murder resulted from a sex game gone wrong. "For sexual violence you need strong proof," she declared. "The prosecution has not provided that to you, and for that reason you cannot convict her."

Del Grosso was right. The evidence of rape was inconclusive—Rudy's DNA was present, but no semen or tears or other signs of forced penetration were found. There was no proof beyond Amanda's well-documented promiscuity that she was a sexual deviant. Amanda's lawyers should have done more to deflate the hype around her louche habits. They sent out a dozen subpoenas for local character witnesses, but only her Greek friend Spyros Gatsios showed up. So Amanda's character witnesses were all from Seattle, and translation inevitably lessens the emotional impact of heartfelt testimony. When her best friend, Madison Paxton, spoke about how honest and innocent Amanda really was, it came across as an emotionless staccato in Italian. Paxton's feelings were, literally, lost in translation.

The other way to address the character issue was to control how Amanda behaved in court. Alessandra Batassa, a criminal lawyer in Rome, once told me: "The jury pays attention to much more than testimony. The lawyers should take control of the client's complete image—including who attends court with her—not just the client's personal behavior." Batassa was shocked to see Amanda come to court in tight jeans and provocative T-shirts; the young woman should have worn conservative clothing, even a dark suit. But Amanda's lawyers left the defense of her character largely to her family, who made their case to American news networks—which, of course, the jury could not see. The jurors saw only Amanda's daily demeanor, which was ill advised.

Amanda herself was probably too honest, confessing in her diaries, which were admissible in court, that she loved sex and enjoyed drugs. During the hearings, she giggled at certain questions. She made a mockery of the judge's court. Smiling to the cameras, blushing, and passing chocolates to Raffaele did little to help her. Bongiorno seemed reluctant to defend Amanda's character until the end of the trial, when the attorney dismissed the theory that the young lovers were looking for new sexual experiences; she called them "love birds in the infancy of their relationship, not some old tired couple looking for new thrills."

The defense's other biggest mistake, according to interviews with jurors after the trial, was doing nothing to refute the mixed-blood evidence beyond noting that it is common to find mingled DNA when two people live in the same house. The jurors needed more than that. "To have mixed blood, you have to both be bleeding," one of them remarked to me after the verdict. "It was obvious that Meredith was bleeding, but why was

Amanda bleeding?" Amanda's lawyers chose not to supply an explanation. Privately, her mother told me she was menstruating. Early in the investigation, her stepfather, Chris Mellas, told a group of reporters that she had an infected ear that had just been pierced. But neither theory was introduced in court.

The defense did a better job trying to prove that the break-in in Filomena Romanelli's room was not staged but the work of an ill-intentioned intruder. The lawyers explained that broken glass might have ended up on top of the scattered clothes because Filomena was allowed to enter the room to check for missing items and may have disturbed things. Still, since Rudy was no stranger to the house, he would have surely known that there was a much easier way into the upper apartment via a back balcony; he didn't have to throw a rock and scale a thirteen-foot wall.

THE PROSECUTION'S CASE might have been defeated had the defense lawyers been more unified. After all, there was no solid confession, no real murder weapon, no convincing motive, and not much evidence. But the lawyers rarely seemed to be on the same page. Bongiorno could not carry the team alone, although she was able to knock down the crucial evidence of the knife through her expert cross-examination. In the last months of the trial, however, Bongiorno rarely even showed up, and when she did, she rarely stayed for the entire hearing. Her state-funded driver in his black Mercedes was always waiting outside the courthouse to whisk her back to the parliament hall in Rome. Meanwhile, Luca Maori, Raffaele's other lawyer, was on trial himself for involuntary manslaughter because he accidentally killed a motorcyclist in a car crash.

Overall, the defense was simply too disjointed. Forensic expert Vincenzo Pascali quit in May, leaving a big hole in the Sollecito team—and a 50,000-euro bill for services rendered. He had been hired to discredit the bra-clasp evidence. But when he started hinting that in his own findings, the sample also contained Knox's DNA, Bongiorno objected. Introducing Amanda's DNA on the specimen would only make things worse, tying both defendants to the crime scene. Instead, she wanted Pascali to focus on contamination, even though it was unlikely that the clasp could have been contaminated with Raffaele's DNA just because it wasn't collected in a timely manner. Unwilling to testify according to the lawyers' script, Pascali walked off the case. He was replaced by Francesco Introna, a close friend of Raffaele's father and a brilliant Pugliese scholar who spoke English to the foreign press. During his testimony, Introna dramatically plunged a knife into the neck of a mannequin to prove his point to the jury. He testified that Meredith was killed by just one person, Rudy Guede, who grabbed her from behind and stabbed her in the neck. A month later, Amanda's own forensic expert, Carlo Torre, told the court that, yes, Meredith had been killed by one person, Rudy Guede, but that she had been stabbed from the front. If the defense experts could not even agree on the details of the murder, what hope was there for the jury to take their side?

Torre is a well-known expert who has authored a string of criminal science textbooks and is a favorite on the international forensic science lecture circuit. With his Albert Einstein hair and frumpy jacket, he was expected to be the highlight of Amanda's defense when he took the stand midway through the trial. But his testimony lacked impact, perhaps because he took such a detached, clinical approach to the evidence, addressing the jurors as if they were pupils who would be tested later.

"You see the wounds on the subject's neck," he said using a red laser pointer on giant autopsy photos of

Meredith. "The larger wound was made by the sawing motion of a smaller knife, not with Exhibit 36," he explained, referring to the knife with Amanda's DNA on the handle. He used a Styrofoam mannequin's head and a knife the same size as Exhibit 36 to demonstrate that point.

"It would have come through the other side," he said, coldly stabbing the mannequin so that the knife blade exited on the far side of her neck. "There is no mystery here. It is not just difficult but it is completely impossible that a knife like this would make these two wounds. The murder weapon is a survival knife, a Rambo knife, not this one," he said, obviously unaware that he was describing most of the knives in Raffaele's extensive collection of tactical knives and switchblades.

TOWARD THE END of the trial, the defense team members tried a make-or-break submission. They insisted that the discrepancies in DNA analysis obliged the judge to order a *superperizia*, or super analyst, to review all the DNA evidence.

"The jury has heard two different explanations for most of the DNA evidence presented," declared Dalla

Vedova. "An independent review will be the final word."

"Rehashing all the evidence will not change its outcome," prosecutor Mignini said, opposing the request. Judge Massei, who always seemed to welcome opportunities to deliberate with his jurors, stood up and, without a word, smiled and led them into chambers. Two hours later, he emerged to say, "I am denying the defense request to have an independent analysis of all the DNA evidence." He added, "The decision is not an indicator of guilt."

But in fact it was. Raffaele sunk in his chair. He knew that the fact that the evidence would stand meant that even the judge believed the prosecution's case. Amanda seemed unaware of the impact of this decision.

The prosecution concluded its final arguments with a video dramatization of the murder, complete with sexy avatars of Amanda, Meredith, Raffaele, and Rudy—the women with big breasts and tiny waists à la Lara Croft, the men with broad shoulders and bulging crotches. It was a bizarre film that superimposed these animated figures over real crime scene photos. Behind the scenes, the making of this video nearly broke the prosecution's team apart. *Il Messaggero*'s Italo

Carmignani learned that Mignini and Comodi clashed over whether to include the sexual violence against Meredith. Mignini also wanted to reintroduce the theory of a Satanic ritual. Comodi blocked both impulses. But the video did prove effective. Rather than listening to defense experts hypothesize with mannequins and diagrams, jurors saw an exact enactment of what the prosecution thought had happened. It was compelling.

THE ANIMATION BEGINS with events that happened late in the afternoon of November 1 and shows Amanda and Raf meeting up with Rudy at the basketball courts. It then jumps from scene to scene according to the time points that were established by witness testimony and logs from the cell phone carrier; a phone that's turned on sends periodic pings to the base station, which can pinpoint its location. There is no dialogue in the video, because the girls would have presumably been speaking English. Instead, prosecutor Comodi reads a narration that includes the time of each segment and an explanation of each scene backed up by courtroom testimony. At 8:18 P.M., Amanda is on the via Ulisse Rocchi in downtown Perugia when she receives a text message from her boss, Patrick, telling her that she didn't have to come in to work. At 8:30, she goes to Raf's apartment on corso Garibaldi nearby. At 8:38, she sends a text to acknowledge Patrick's message. Meanwhile, Meredith is finishing dinner with her English friends. At 8:45 P.M., she and Sophie leave Robyn's house, then split up at the via Roscetto. At 8:46 P.M., Raf turns off his cell phone. At 9 P.M., the video shows, Meredith is eating a mushroom out of the fridge back at her apartment. (There were no mushrooms on the pizza at Robyn's house, yet it was the last food she ate, according to autopsy reports. But there was no sign that this could have been a hallucinogenic.) Raffaele makes the last keystroke on his computer at 9:10 P.M. At 9:45, the video shows, Amanda and Raffaele leave his apartment and head toward the basketball courts on Piazza Grimana to reach via della Pergola. At Amanda's house, they meet Rudy to work out a prearranged drug deal. At 11:20, Amanda opens the door on via della Pergola, and the three enter the apartment.

Meredith is in her room. Rudy goes into the bathroom while Amanda and Raffaele confront Meredith, teasing and taunting her. Suddenly, Amanda turns aggressive. A physical fight breaks out between the two girls, and the video shows Amanda first grabbing Meredith's throat and then shoving the palm of her hand against Meredith's chin to push her head against the wall, knocking her unconscious—and here the video superimposes actual shots of Meredith's bruises to show how they match the size and shape of Amanda's animated hand. Rudy enters the room just before Meredith falls to the floor. Amanda, Raf, and Rudy undress her, first pulling down her blue jeans and underwear and then pushing her T-shirt above her breasts. Then Meredith comes to. Raf pulls his switchblade out of his pocket, and a few minutes later, Amanda runs to the kitchen to get another knife. Meredith uses her right hand to fight back, which causes the tiny knife wounds on the palms of her hands. Raf tries to unhook Meredith's bra but fails to work the clasp; he slices it off her later, after she's been stabbed. Meredith falls to her knees. Amanda then directs Rudy and Raffaele to hold Meredith's arms back. Rudy reaches down to touch Meredith's vagina. Amanda holds the larger knife to Meredith's neck, teasing her with it and dancing it across her neck, leaving fine cuts. Raffaele holds his knife against the other side of her neck from behind. Amanda then plunges the knife into Meredith's neck and she utters the scream heard by elderly neighbor Nara Capezzali. Blood sprays on the wardrobe, and Meredith falls to the ground. Then the three assailants pull Meredith to the side of her bed, and again, the avatar's movement is superimposed over crime scene photos of the blood smear left by her hair across the floor. Rudy ministers to Meredith, who is coughing and spitting blood. Amanda and Raf grab Meredith's phones and run from the apartment, leaving Rudy and the dying Meredith.

The video was compelling about the mechanics of the murder, but less convincing on the subject of motive. This has always been the weakest link in the prosecution's case, and in fact their theory of the crime changed several times over the course of the investigation. In the days right after the murder, there was talk of a Satanic ritual because of the Halloween paraphernalia found at the girls' villa and Raf's apartment. That hypothesis was soon discounted, however, and replaced with the idea of sex games gone wrong in a fog of drugs and alcohol. Unfortunately, no alcohol or drug testing was immediately done on Amanda, Raf, or Rudy, and Meredith's initial toxicology reports showed that she had had no more than a glass of wine. (Later toxicology reports showed that she may have been very drunk, but the prosecution wrote those off as bad forensics—they said her body had not been stored properly, so the blood alcohol levels were due to fermentation, not intoxication. As for Amanda and Raf, when they were finally arrested, on November 6, only the slightest unidentifiable trace of narcotics was found through hair samples—not even enough to identify the substance.) By the time the case reached court, however, the idea of sex games with Meredith as a willing participant had evolved into a notion of conflict between the two roommates that provoked Amanda and the two men to sexually taunt and assault her. This was the motivation assumed in the video reenactment, with a voiceover by prosecutor Comodi explaining that the narcissistic Amanda had total control of the situation.

MY OWN VIEW IS THAT the video is too harsh, because it does not credit the role of drugs and alcohol in the events of that night. Although prosecutor Mignini mentioned drugs in his closing arguments—specifically, heroin, cocaine, and acid in addition to the superenhanced cannabis common on the back streets of Perugia—the prosecution video never shows Amanda, Raf, and Rudy getting high, and the avatars appear to be in control of themselves, acting with intentional cruelty. The more likely scenario, if Amanda and Raf are truly guilty in Meredith's death, is that they were so blasted that they had lost touch with their own rational selves—and truly cannot recall exactly what happened that night. This could have been the dangerous side effect of their budding romance: According to Amanda's prison diaries, Raf had been reminiscing about his incredible highs on heroin and cocaine, and she may have been eager to try it; she in turn might have introduced him to "hard A"—the high-proof mix of liquors popular with college students in the Pacific Northwest. By sharing their knowledge, two experienced thrill seekers could have found a way to get higher than ever—with lethal consequences.

Consider this scenario: Although they never admitted it in court, it is entirely plausible that Amanda and Raf saw Rudy at the basketball courts during their late afternoon walk on November 1. They placed an order for drugs, which Rudy then delivered to via della Pergola around 9 P.M., just as Meredith was getting home. But she was tired from her late Halloween night and had no interest in getting high. Amanda and Raf, however, were planning to be higher than usual—too high to take phone calls, particularly from Raf's dad, who'd already threatened him with rehab. Records show both their phones were turned off around 8:30.

Between 9:15 and 11:15, Amanda, Raf, and Rudy got themselves seriously messed up; Amanda asked Meredith if she could lend her money to pay Rudy, and Meredith reluctantly did so. (This explains why three hundred euros Meredith had withdrawn to pay her rent was missing and there was a trace of Rudy's DNA mixed with her blood on the zipper of the handbag but only her fingerprints on the wallet. She got the money out herself. Later, after the murder, Rudy, covered in her blood, probably moved her purse from the floor onto the bed. But he and Amanda and Raf were all acquitted of robbery.) Meredith was angry about having to lend Amanda money and retired to her room. Things were tense between the two roommates, and at a certain level of intoxication, it seemed like a good idea to Amanda to start baiting her. She prodded Rudy to go see Meredith; he went to her bedroom and started trying to kiss her and fondle her until she called out. Amanda and Raffaele went back to see what was going on, and instead of helping Meredith fend off Rudy, joined in the taunting. Actual rape was never confirmed in this case, but Rudy did violate Meredith with his fingers before, during, or after the murder. His DNA traces were found inside her vagina, but they were not from semen or blood.

By this point, Amanda, Raf, and Rudy were beyond the control of conscience. Raf took a switchblade out of his pocket and started teasing Meredith with it. Rudy had a knife in his backpack, and that came out as well. They had no intention of killing Meredith, but they were taunting her with knives on each side of her neck and she, in essence, impaled herself on the larger knife as she twisted in the grip of someone holding back her arms. Her final scream was the one Nara heard. When they realized what they had done, the three assailants panicked. They first tried to save her, taking a towel and putting it on the biggest wound, but they all freaked out and ran out of the apartment and up the metal steps in the parking garage below Nara's apartment. Rudy headed out into the night, taking Meredith's cell phones and his knife with him. A young couple would later testify that they had seen a frantic black man running away from the direction of the via della Pergola that night. Rudy threw the cell phones over a hedge and kept the knife, eventually dumping it when he was on the lam in Germany.

Amanda and Raffaele ditched the pocketknife and eventually went back to the house, first looking at the villa from the basketball courts where Antonio Curatolo, the homeless man, saw them. They went to Amanda's room and passed out.

THE NEXT MORNING, Amanda and Raffaele wake up around 6:00 A.M. with crippling hangovers and no memories of the night before. They peek into Meredith's room to find her battered and lifeless body, but they still can't remember anything. The broken glass on Meredith's floor that no one was ever able to explain was from liquor bottles. Amanda and Raf have blood on their hands, and they begin to panic. First, they both turn on their cell phones about 6:30 A.M. to see if their messages offer any clues. They do not; Amanda's last text is to Patrick Lumumba about work the night before, Raf's phone shows both a missed call and a text message—both from his father. Rudy is nowhere to be found, and in fact, they don't remember that he was there. Amanda had a hazy recollection of a black man, but the only person she can think of is Patrick.

Although they can't remember exactly what happened the night before, obviously a dead body means trouble. If the police suspect Raf and Amanda had anything to do with it, they will surely be drug-tested, which risks not only charges for serious drugs but also the wrath of Dr. Sollecito. Not thinking clearly, they convince themselves that they can clean up the house, stage a break-in, retreat to Raf's apartment, and claim total ignorance—which, given their blackouts, isn't entirely a lie. At some point, Raffaele goes to shower, leaving his bloody bare footprint on the bathmat and another in the hallway. Amanda doesn't shower at all. In the photos from that morning, her makeup is smudged, and the cops whisper about her body odor. She changes clothes and puts her bloody socks and other clothing in a plastic shopping bag to throw away. Amanda's bare footprints, most likely left in blood, were later turned up in the hallway with Luminol. Around 7:30 A.M., the couple leaves the apartment to buy cleaning supplies. Raffaele wants to change his clothes, so he goes home while Amanda goes to the store. Marco Quintavalle, the owner of the Conad store near Raf's house, testified that Amanda was waiting at his store when he opened at 7:45.

RETURNING TO Amanda's apartment, Amanda and Raf start cleaning up. To simulate a break-in, Raf pulls the clothing out of Filomena's drawers and then opens the casement window so he can throw a rock through it from inside the room. He forgets to open the shutters, which first tips off the officers to the idea of a staged break-in. Amanda, who had been cleaning the bathroom, comes into Filomena's room at some point, leaving the incriminating drop of mixed DNA and blood on the floor. Raffaele notices it and wipes it up, but Luminol will bring it back to light. They start the washing machine, adding some of Amanda's clothes to the pile in Meredith's laundry basket—although Amanda would later testify that she never used the house washing machine. The machine is still warm when the police arrive after noon. Amanda and Raf do a pretty good job of wiping the house clean—police note an unusual absence of fingerprints—but in their haste, they neglect several drops of blood in the bathroom the girls shared.

When they go back to Meredith's room, however, they are overwhelmed. They know better than to leave tracks there, so they put on shoes and stand on towels to scoot into the room, which explains the smudges on the floor. Amanda, in her testimony, actually described this ruse in response to a prosecutor's question about why there were no bare footprints in her own bedroom even though she said she was in there after her shower. She explained that she had not wanted to get the floor wet, so she used her towel as a sort of magic carpet. The defense later maintained that the few bare footprints and sneaker prints in Meredith's room all belonged to Rudy, without adequately explaining why he would have one shoe on and one shoe off. It makes more sense to think that Rudy had his shoes on and Raf, who was more comfortable in the house, had his off.

This may be when Amanda decides she can't look at Meredith's open eyes any longer. Meredith's corpse is between Amanda and the bed. She is uneasy as she reaches over Meredith and pulls the duvet off the bed to cover her; in doing so, Amanda loses her balance and steps off the towel, putting an unstable foot on the pillow underneath Meredith's body—how else explain the bloody footprint on the pillow consistent with Amanda's shoe size? There are no similar prints elsewhere in the room, only smudges on the floor. Amanda and Raf then wipe most, but not all, of the surface prints around the room—including everything on the outside door handle, which raises the question of how anyone exited the room and locked it from the outside. A few of the missed fingerprints in Meredith's room are later matched to Rudy, but there are only a few; the remaining fourteen unidentifiable finger-prints inside the room are probably his and Amanda's and Raf's.

By now it is nearly noon. Amanda, feeling shaky and paranoid, calls the person she trusts most in the world—her mom—at 4 A.M. Seattle time. She says that something strange has happened in the house. Then Raf goes to dump the empty liquor bottles and clean-ing bottles and bloody clothes and rags in one of the silver dumpsters in town. When he returns, Amanda has just walked out into the yard to empty the mop bucket that they generally dumped on the driveway gravel rather than down the sink. That's why she doesn't have a jacket on and Raf does when the postal police arrive with Meredith's phones.

The hazy, disjointed statements about that night Amanda later makes to police suggest a genuine black-out; a purposeful lie would certainly be more coher-ent. Despite immense pressure, neither Amanda nor Raf has ever broken and told the "real story," because they truly don't remember it. Rudy, on the other hand, remembers enough to tell the appeals judge he "sees red" every time he closes his eyes. But whether he was less stoned than Amanda and Raf, an instigator of Meredith's torture, or someone who went along, only Rudy can say.

9

"Deep Down, Curt Knows. He Knows the Truth"

AMANDA KNOX'S FAMILY has been heroic in support of their daughter. If sheer effort and blind faith were sufficient to overturn a murder charge, she would surely be a free woman by now. Her parents have driven themselves into bankruptcy to fund her legal and public relations teams. Family members camped in Perugia in shifts, staying at an inexpensive *agriturismo* near the prison outside town, driving a cheap Fiat, and bringing in canned soups and packaged meals from the United States to eat cheaply when they weren't being wined and dined by the American networks. But in their disregard for appearances and local mores, they sometimes hurt Amanda's case while trying to help her.

Edda Mellas, an elementary-school math teacher, was the most popular of Amanda's four parents and stepparents. Her husband, Chris Mellas, an Internet consultant for a Schnitzer development company in Seattle, was the least. He spent each hearing on his BlackBerry, reading news stories and firing off vile, unsigned hate mail to journalists and bloggers. Chris rarely looked at Amanda, even when she spoke — and, unlike the other family members, he didn't go back to the dungeon to hug her at the end of each session.

"That *patrigno*," Guiliano Mignini said to me during a courtroom break, nodding toward Chris. "*Qualcosa non va* — Something not right about him." Mignini liked to talk about Amanda's family. He had analyzed their phone intercepts and their body language in the courtroom. He thought Amanda's father, Curt Knox, who was a vice president for finance at Macy's until he was laid off in 2009, was "the smart one."

"He is different from the rest," Mignini often said. "Deep down, Curt knows. He knows the truth."

A father of three daughters himself, Mignini understood why Curt wanted to believe in Amanda. But the lawyer also saw something in Curt that only those who spent a lot of time in the courtroom had noticed. Curt was angry, his face often red as he stifled his tears. But he knew how he was expected to act. In the waning days of the trial, Curt's wife Cassandra slipped in her high-heeled boots and fell to the ground in front of Mignini. As Mignini helped her up, Curt stammered a *grazie* to the man who was trying to convict his daughter of murder.

Curt may have the brains, but Edda carried the family. She wasn't a celebrity like her daughter, but a mother's love is not something taken lightly in Italy. She cried constantly, painfully, honestly. Her eyes were red-rimmed, her puffy face permanently blotchy. She is the martyr of this saga; she is also a good person. Even when she knows she should, she simply cannot hate people, though she was well-versed in the family's enemies list. On one sticky July afternoon, she and her cousin Dorothy Craft Najir, who lives in Hamburg, approached the gaggle of reporters "de-Knoxing" amiably at the outdoor tables of the Brufani Hotel bar. Stories filed, video transmitted, most of us were bent over a BlackBerry or cell phone, texting husbands, wives, lovers, and editors after a long day in court. The main topic of conversation was how to nab press tickets to James Taylor's Umbrian jazz concert the next night.

Edda and Dorothy checked out the group. Two family favorites, Chapman Bell of NBC and Sabina

Castelfranco of CBS, were there, but they were sitting with the "axis of evil"—British tabloid reporter Nick Pisa and me. So Edda and Dorothy walked on. Later, over the usual network-paid dinner, Edda asked Chapman how she could possibly stand to be around us. This trial is Edda's life, of course, not just another story, so she cannot fathom how we can all write and say such different things about her daughter, yet still be friends. What she didn't understand is that the TV reporters' honest views were not that different from those of the print press—but TV people had to toe the party line to get the family on camera. The TV producers would sometimes send text messages to find out where the unfriendlies were—so they could avoid us while they were with the family and know where to hook up later. It was a touchy situation that everyone understood. There can be no hard feelings when it comes to the politics of access.

Yet after the network meal, mellowed by wine, Edda, rather than return to the *agriturismo*, would sometimes choose to tag along with her dinner hosts to see what happened next. One night, early in the trial, she came with two TV reporters to the Joyce Pub, where the foreign press routinely gathered for nightcaps and shop talk. We all sat at a back table littered with shot glasses and beer bottles. Everyone had had too much to drink. Leaning over Nick Pisa, Edda held my hand and pleaded with us to believe in Amanda. "She is innocent," she says, her eyes welling up.

A few months later, on a far more sober occasion, Edda and I sit together over lemon sodas on corso Vannucci. "My family would *kill* me if they knew I was meeting you," she says, missing the irony of the threat. Then she tells me that I had been the worst, one of the very worst, to write "these lies and leaks" about Amanda.

"Like what?" I ask. "What did I write that wasn't true?"

Her phone rings. It is Madison Paxton, Amanda's best friend, who is spending the summer with her in Perugia. They talk for a few minutes and then hang up.

"Madison says I should spit on you," Edda says, laughing apologetically. "She's just young. She doesn't understand this stuff."

"So what have I written that is not true?" I ask again.

"I've never read your stories," she says. "Chris just tells me that you are the worst."

We talk about the sex scandal involving Italian Prime Minister Silvio Berlusconi. Italy is buzzing about the orgies at his summer home, and I use my

BlackBerry to send Edda the link to an *El País* newspaper story that shows the Czech prime minister, nude and sexually aroused, at Berlusconi's Sardinian villa.

"I don't understand how he can cheat on his wife like that," she says about Berlusconi. "What's wrong with this society where men think it is OK to have affairs?"

She frowns. Maybe she is thinking of Curt, who left her for Cassandra, when Edda was pregnant with Deanna. But she shrugs and happily goes back to gossiping about Berlusconi's orgies. I dish more dirt, and we giggle like girlfriends. Then she remembers I'm the enemy.

OF ALL THE FAMILY, Edda spent the most time in Perugia, especially in the summer on her school vacation. During the hottest months, when the *aula* became stifling, she, Madison, and her daughter Deanna Knox would sometimes come upstairs to the small, crowded room assigned to the press, which had a video feed from the court, and sit making snide comments as the journalists tried to work.

But after Curt lost his job at Macy's, he started to show up more. Even though they were divorced, Edda and Curt did their best to present a unified front in supporting Amanda, but it was hard on their spouses to see the former couple together so often. Countless rumors circulated in Perugia about how Curt and Chris had to keep their wives apart when they were all in town for the verdict. When any of the four parents came to Perugia alone, they often brought a friend of Amanda's. Chris Mellas came with Amanda's Seattle boyfriend, DJ, and the two men spent most of their time chewing tobacco and drinking beer with Frank the blogger. Edda often brought Madison and Deanna. During the summer, she also brought one of Curt and Cassandra's daughters, fourteen-year-old Ashley Knox. (Their youngest daughter, eleven-year-old Delaney, stayed in Seattle.) It was a hot summer, and the Seattle girls spent their time at the *agriturismo* swimming pool when they weren't at hearings or visiting Amanda. They were courted by the local press, and at one point promised favorable coverage in an Italian weekly women's magazine in exchange for access. Trusting the friendly gesture, the girls made a serious error in judgment: They posed around Perugia for a photo spread in *Gente*, the Italian version of *People* magazine. The most damning photo—of Deanna and Ashley in short-shorts, leaning on a metal fence outside "the house of horrors"—was seen as a slap in the face to the Kerchers, and they were lambasted in the British press for treating the scene of Meredith's murder as a tourist attraction.

Edda also misread the intentions of a media suitor when the family granted blanket access to a documentary film crew from Britain's Channel 4. The producer, Garfield Kennedy, and his crew became the family's personal entourage, accompanying them to each prison meeting and press interview during the trial. At one point, the documentary was to be called *Making a Killing*—about how the press created the hype around Meredith's murder—and Edda told me that Garfield was doing "a real nice documentary about us." But when the one-hour show aired in January 2010, it confirmed what a strange young woman Amanda was. "She's a very quirky person. She's not normal," her best friend Madison said on camera. "She is a little bit odd," Amanda's Seattle boyfriend, DJ, agreed. "She's really not conventional at all," he said. "She's not tied down by social standards." It also showed how media-hungry the family had become. In the opening segment, in the Mellas home in Seattle, the camera shows Edda directing Deanna to turn on the big-screen television. The mother's eyes light up as

Deanna shouts from the TV room, "Amanda's on GMA!"

The Knoxes are honest people who did what any parents would. But they couldn't help getting caught up in their sudden fame; by the end of the trial, they were skilled at attaching their own mics, counting for the technicians in New York, and then speaking in sound bites. Edda was a guaranteed on-camera crier—always good TV. Chris was not allowed to give interviews, and the producers knew that even if he volunteered, he was not to be put on camera—strict orders from PR adviser David Marriott in Seattle. Curt, on the other hand, gave seamless answers, and he, too, could tear up on demand. Marriott brokered the on-camera appearances and tried desperately to control the message by meting out access according to which networks painted Amanda in the best light. To a large extent, he was successful; Knox was always referred to in TV reports as "honor student Amanda Knox" (true), and correspondents frequently mentioned that there was "no evidence linking her to the crime scene" (only true if you limit the crime scene to Meredith's room and demand a 100 percent certain match for shoe prints and marks on the body). Marriott frequently demanded that written dispatches from

181

the courtroom be removed from the network Web sites if they were not completely Amanda-friendly. In one showdown with a network, he threatened to deny access to Edda unless an item was deleted, but the network did not back down and Edda was again on camera a few weeks later. After the verdict, Marriott told producers that the family would not appear on any program if I was also a guest, because I had declared on CNN's *Anderson Cooper 360°* that I thought Amanda got a fair trial.

Unfortunately, no one paid that much attention to controlling the family's untelevised appearances in Perugia—in front of the people who would decide Amanda's fate. Deanna and Ashley also wore their short-shorts and tank tops to hearings. Curt in his Hawaiian shirts and Chris in his slick suits and military haircut might not have fit in with the stylish Italian men, but they did not offend the court. Edda and the girls were another story. Italy is a country where women dress seductively, but they rarely bare their thighs—shorts are for the beach. The court of justice is an esteemed institution. On more than one occasion, friendly members of the press whispered to Edda that her daughters would be well advised to cover up their bare shoulders and tuck in their bra straps or wear more appropriate dresses. Edda always defended her daughters' attire by pointing out that officials in the courtroom wore tight pants and low-cut sweaters. Detective Monica Napoleoni and Stefania the stenographer, whose short skirts and sequined tops were the talk of the press room, were hardly conservative dressers—but they weren't in court to support someone on trial for murder. After the verdict, jurors said they thought the Knox family appeared arrogant in the courtroom. Edda and the others continued to "be themselves" when they should have tried harder to respect local customs in a country where image counts for so much. Edda once told a morning news program that her lawyers told them "to just be who we are." Those same lawyers told me that they could not get the family to cooperate.

"They don't understand," Amanda's assistant attorney Maria del Grosso once told me over breakfast at the Fortuna Hotel. "They can't see beyond the immediate urgency of their situation. They can't see the big picture."

Nor, it seems, could David Marriott, who apparently did not anticipate how ill-advised American editorials based on his very partial and partisan information would play in Italy. A decade ago, many major newspapers would have dispatched a correspondent to Perugia on a story like this, but with the economic pinch, the number of foreign correspondents on the ground in Italy has dwindled dramatically, and those few are often responsible for Spain, Greece, and North Africa as well. Even the Associated Press had a difficult time staffing all the hearings, because of budget constraints. So most U.S. papers covered the trial from afar, and it was much simpler to quote the family and pipe information from Marriott than to wade through volumes of Italian court documents.

Even the *New York Times* fell prey to Knox family propaganda. In June, as the prosecution was wrapping up, blogger Timothy Egan lambasted Italy's derelict justice system: "The case against Knox has so many holes in it, and is so tied to the career of a powerful Italian prosecutor who is under indictment for professional misconduct, that any fair-minded jury would have thrown it out months ago." He declared the trial a "railroad job from hell"—citing the authority of CBS legal analyst Paul Ciolino, who had been to Perugia in the early days of the investigation. But Egan never came to Italy for a hearing or read any court documents. If he had, he might not have made such basic mistakes as getting the number of jurors wrong or substantially misrepresenting Rudy Guede's role. (Another part of the pro-Amanda brief was that since Guede had already been convicted of the murder, it was a horrible miscarriage of justice to keep prosecuting Amanda and Raf.) Egan also dredged up the dead issue of Mignini's obsession with Satanism, even though that angle was never introduced in court. Egan's piece was widely picked up across Italy, where he was criticized for his pious, uninformed views. The *New York Times* regular Rome-based correspondent, Rachel Donadio, made it to only a few hearings over the course of the trial. But when she came, she was greeted with great hostility in Perugia, despite her efforts to report accurately on the proceedings, in blatant contradiction to Egan's blogs.

THE VERDICT CAME DOWN after midnight on December 5, 2009. The local police had grossly underestimated the number of reporters on the scene and ended up herding us forcibly—and painfully— through the narrow wooden doors into the courthouse. The cameras were relegated to the press room; print press were allowed in court after showing the police officers that our cell phones were turned off so there would be no rogue photos when the verdict was read. Curt, Edda, Chris, and Cassandra and all their daughters were there. So were Raffaele's father, stepmother, and sister. As at a wedding, the *innocentisti* press stood behind Amanda's family. I stood behind Meredith's— Arline, John, and their other children, Stephanie, John Jr., and Lyle, who sat with a representative from the British Embassy. When Amanda walked in for the last time, there were no cameras to snap her picture. No one yelled questions. The judge and jury came in solemnly. Two of the women jurors were crying. It was well understood by then what the judge would say. He took a deep breath before he read the word *"condannato"* for Amanda Marie Knox. Both she and Raffaele were convicted of the crimes of sexual assault, murder, and staging a crime scene; Amanda was additionally convicted of defaming Patrick Lumumba. Amanda began to weep. Her family did not understand the Italian statement, and only when they saw Amanda react did their worst fears come true. Deanna's cries filled the courtroom. Edda wept in silence. Curt's anger was palpable. Chris seemed oblivious. Raffaele's father shook his head, tears streaming down his face. His stepmother yelled out "Fuck you!" and then "Be strong,

Raffaele" into the courtroom. Arline Kercher turned her whole body to stare at Edda Mellas; John put his hand on her shoulder. Raffaele began to shake as he cried. Amanda wept in Luciano Ghirga's arms before the guards took her away. There were no hugs in the dungeon, and this time, the two convicted killers rode back to prison in separate vans.

Then no one knew quite what to do. David Marriott had not bothered coming to Perugia, and his clients were left to fight their way through the media scrum unprotected. Edda and Deanna escaped quickly and ran down the street to a waiting car that whisked them to the Brufani hotel. Curt clung to Ashley and Delaney, pushing away cameramen as he tried to leave the building. When Curt and his two daughters finally made it out of the old wooden doors, they heard the cries "Assassins, assassins" as the two paddy wagons drove past the front of the courthouse, blue lights flashing into the night. Then, in a surreal moment, Curt, Ashley, and Delaney marched, heads high, down the corso Vannuci to the Brufani hotel, a crush of cameras following them like the tail of a kite. Documentary filmmaker Garfield Kennedy was in front of Curt, shooting back toward the crowd, getting the shot he was waiting for. Safely inside the Brufani, the family regrouped in their network-funded suites and sat for interviews with the favored correspondents.

Back in United States, there was an intemperate, jingoistic burst of outrage from the people who knew about the trial only through Knox-approved dispatches. Journalist Judy Bachrach, who had traveled to Perugia for *Vanity Fair* for a preliminary hearing, which had been closed to the press, described the case against Knox as "a magic show filled with testimony about Amanda's vibrator and condoms, and empty of proof" even though she never attended the actual trial. Seattle Senator Maria Cantwell threatened diplomatic action. (Never mind that the U.S. Embassy in Rome, as well as international human rights groups, had decided early on that the case was legitimate and did not merit extraordinary intervention, although the embassy did send observers to the trial.) Donald Trump and hundreds of other people with comments on the *New York Times* Web site vowed to boycott Italy. Naturally, Italians found this all deeply insulting. It took several days before the outcry quit drowning out the more reasonable voices observing that, given the evidence in the case, Amanda would probably have been convicted in an American court as well. That was followed by Amanda's own comment after the verdict, to a member of Italian parliament touring the prison: "Yes, the system was fair to me." (The family tried to deny she'd said it.)

The Knox clan hung around for a few days after the verdict, and the networks continued their courtship, all for the ultimate get—a prison interview with Amanda. But eight days after the verdict, two wire service reporters sneaked into the prison under the flag of a joint Italian-American foundation and got the exclusive first tidbit.

"I'm scared," Amanda told Patricia Thomas of the Associated Press. "I don't know what is going on." It wasn't the interview that everyone wanted. Thomas was not even able to ask about the trial; still, it lessened the value of those first jailhouse words. Marriott and the family have hinted that they will not give anyone an interview until the appeal process begins—in effect dangling the carrot to keep the networks interested and their coverage positive.

The family had been optimistic that Amanda would be acquitted and even bought a plane ticket for her to come home. Edda had planned a spa day for her back in Seattle, and Marriott was already brokering book and movie deals. Instead, Edda stayed until Christmas

Eve. On her first attempt to visit Amanda after the verdict, the mother was denied access to Capanne prison. Now that Amanda was a convicted murderer, the rules changed and the visits were limited to just six a month.

10

"You Try to Be Persuasive but Not Insulting"

For THE THIRD YEAR in a row, Amanda Knox had the lead part in the Christmas play at Capanne prison outside Perugia. She played the blue-eyed Virgin Mary in a solemn religious pageant performed under the direction of the prison chaplain. But her long-running role on the international stage has ended, for now. Since December 5, when she was convicted of murdering Meredith Kercher, Amanda has lost the distraction of her weekly outings to court, each one a star turn before a ravenous media. Now, she is just another inmate, moved to the felony wing of the prison. Her previous cell mates—a Roma gypsy, a Chinese immigrant, and a woman from Kosovo who was on trial for killing her boyfriend—have been replaced by a fifty-three-year-old American drug pusher from New Orleans serving a four-year sentence. Amanda's next hope for an outing is when her appeal is heard, most likely in the fall of 2010.

Amanda is fighting the demons that come with incarceration—depression, anxiety, paranoia, and hopelessness. Her hair is falling out under the stress. She is haunted by insomnia. Her dreams keep her awake. Her family will not authorize a jailhouse interview because of her fragile psychological state. Her family has been fairly successful at controlling how Amanda is portrayed, at least in U.S. media, but they have never been able to control how she presents herself. Amanda never quite fit the family's script of a naive honor student, and now she has been in prison for more than two years, learning to negotiate the tricky politics of life in a population of murderers, drug addicts, and thieves. Gone is the whimsical girl who felt confident enough to perform cartwheels in a police station. She is taking correspondence courses at the University of Washington to finish her degree, but she has no access to e-mail, so she has to rely on the Italian postal system to turn in her schoolwork. An avid linguist who came to Europe to study German and Italian, she is now teaching herself Chinese and Russian. She gets an hour of outdoor recreation each day. She can visit the prison beauty salon once a week. She is on the waiting list to work in the laundry. The money she makes there can be spent on treats such as writing paper, candy bars, and cigarettes, which she can trade for even better stuff like music CDs and smuggled drugs. She gets just six visits a month from family members, who can bring her certain items of food and clothing.

Amanda is still very much her own person, not inclined to give much thought to the consequences of her actions. She writes uncensored letters from prison to whomever she wants. She speaks freely to anyone who walks past her cell. Prison administrators see a certain value in letting visitors swing by her cell block to get a look at Capanne's biggest celebrity, and the family has no control over that. In the days after the verdict, a local Umbrian lawmaker visited Capanne and just happened upon Amanda's cell. Later, he reported that she told him that she still had faith in the Italian judicial system and that her trial was "correct." Amanda's family quickly shot down those comments as "misconstrued." After all, how could they justify the media maelstrom in America if Amanda actually believed she got a fair trial in Italy?

Amanda's family is increasingly desperate both to keep the story alive and to keep it under their control.

But putting her on camera is risky. If Amanda were to appear mentally unstable or repeat some of her early recollections of being in the house when Meredith was murdered, it would hurt her already fragile public image. And to compound the potential problems, both Amanda and her parents have now been sued for defamation for claiming that the Perugia police brutalized her during their interrogation. In an interview they gave to John Follain of the *Sunday Times* of London, Curt and Edda repeated Amanda's claims that she had been given no food or water for nine hours and threatened and beaten by the police. They were served papers at lawyer Luciano Ghirga's office when they arrived in Perugia on November 27, 2009, for closing arguments in their daughter's case. Amanda's lawyers never lodged an official complaint for the alleged police brutality, even though Edda told me last summer that they promised her they would do it right after the verdict, no matter how that went. But the lawyers let it go, so the police saw a chance to clear their name. In January 2010, Amanda was served notice in her prison cell. She, too, is being charged for testifying that police hit her on the back of the head twice. After months of hostile publicity, the Perugian authorities are sensitive to criticism. But the family is wary, too; it would be extremely risky right now to have Amanda pressed by a tough investigative journalist looking for ratings.

AMANDA'S FAMILY HAS mortgaged both the Knox and the Mellas family homes and borrowed against their pensions. They have held frequent fund-raisers and accepted donations of both cash and frequent-flyer points on the Amanda Defense Fund Web site (www.amandadefensefund.org). Curt, who lost his job at Macy's last summer, has not yet found new work. On top of legal fees, Amanda's family has the added burden of international travel. Edda has hinted that she would move to Perugia if she could find reasonable employment as a teacher or translator. For now, Curt, Edda, Chris, and Edda's brother still come in shifts. But if Amanda loses her appeals, it seems unlikely they will be able to sustain this schedule for years and years.

Raffaele Sollecito's parents are extremely wealthy, so they have not been substantially harmed by the costs of his defense. But they believe, passionately, that their son suffered from being tried together with Knox, and they may move to sever the two cases on appeal.

Raffaele's lawyer, Giulia Bongiorno, admitted that she started working on the appeal on the trip back to Rome the night of the verdict. The risk she took to mount a joint defense had failed her. On appeal, she has hinted, she may go it alone. The evidence against Raf was far less damning than that against Amanda, and, as is Bongiorno's habit, she sent out drones to interview jurists and determine precisely what happened in the judge's chambers. What she learned confirmed her initial sense that Raffaele was a more sympathetic figure without Amanda. The appeal may well prove her right.

The priority for the Sollecitos is getting Raffaele off suicide watch. Since the verdict, he has been increasingly withdrawn. He is in the sex offenders' ward at Capanne, and like most of the inmates there, he is on heavy antidepressants. He has given up his studies, and his family says he has also given up hope. He has stopped writing letters to his daily newspaper, and he barely responds when his family comes to visit him. He knows enough about the Italian justice system to understand that his chances of getting off on the first round of appeal are slim. The thought of spending four or five years until the second level of appeal is too much for him to bear. His family is petitioning to have him moved closer to them in Puglia, but the prisons in the south are much rougher.

In Italy, the appeal process is complex and involves two levels. A full acquittal is rarely won on the first round, even though a full 50 percent of all cases are won on the second and final stage of the appeal. On the first round, the appeals judge can choose to overturn the conviction entirely or to uphold the decision and simply increase or reduce the sentence. In Rudy Guede's appeal, which was heard around the same time that closing arguments were being made in Amanda and Raffaele's trial, the judge chose to uphold the initial ruling; he agreed that Rudy murdered Meredith Kercher along with Amanda and Raffaele. But Rudy did win a reduction in his sentence from thirty to sixteen years for what the judge called "extenuating factors," not least of which was his cooperation in placing Amanda and Raffaele at the crime scene.

Amanda and Raffaele can only begin their appeal process after Judge Massei's reasoning, or *motivazione*, is released from the Corte d'Assise. The deadline is strict—Massei must file his report within ninety days of the verdict—and few Italian judges rush the deadline, determined to ensure that the person they have convicted serves the most time possible in the event his or her verdict is overturned. Judge Massei's statement is expected in early March. After it is delivered, defense lawyers have forty-five days to officially file their appeal. There is very little they can do without first studying the intricacies of the judge's reasoning. Even the slightest misstep by Judge Massei could give the defense a loophole to crawl through. The first-level appeals judge is from a higher Italian court than Judge Massei. This higher judge will review all the evidence and testimony from the first trial with a more highly qualified jury. In the initial case, the jury members only had to have a junior high school diploma. In the first appeal, they must be high school diploma or equivalent.

If Amanda and Raffaele lose in the first appeal round, their cases are automatically pushed to Italy's highest *cassazione* court, where they have a better chance at a reversal. This level more closely corresponds to a U.S. appeals court; it does not retry the facts of the case, but focuses only on points of law, closely examining any procedural errors made during the investigation and trial. Did the evidence in the Knox case pass all *legal* requirements? The knife, surely not. Nor did the sneaker footprint that initially landed Raf in jail. The highest court must also examine the definition of each accusation. In Italy, first-degree murder requires motivation, yet Amanda, Raffaele, and Rudy were convicted without solid proof of a motive, by the prosecution's own admission. The law also requires that an autopsy must conclusively point to sexual assault for a conviction on that charge, yet that was never medically proven in Meredith's case.

It can take several years, however, for the case to finally be resolved at the highest level. Most legal observers in Italy predict that an acquittal at the high court level would be the best outcome: The presumed killers would have paid a price—in jail time and legal expenses—and the police and prosecutors would pay for their various sloppy mistakes. But the litmus test, of course, is what happens to Rudy. His murder conviction will be the first of the three to be heard by the high court. If he is acquitted, it is likely that Amanda and Raffaele also will go home, too. If he is not, then chances are that his partners in crime will stay in jail as well.

A month after the verdict, Amanda's supporters declared that her defense team had been bolstered with Philadelphia lawyer Theodore Simon, a popular legal analyst for U.S. TV networks who specializes in Americans caught in foreign legal systems. He represented high school student Michael Fay, who was sentenced to prison and public lashings in Singapore for vandalism. Simon got the nine lashings reduced to four and won Fay a reprieve from hard prison time. He also represented Ira Einhorn—the so-called Unicorn Killer—a Philadelphia New Age guru who killed his young girlfriend and stored her in a trunk in his apartment. While Einhorn was on the lam in Europe for many years, he was convicted, in absentia, of the murder. When he was finally apprehended in France in 1997, Simon managed to block his extradition by arguing that a conviction in absentia violated Einhorn's human rights. But in 2001, Einhorn was finally extradited to the United States and is currently serving a life sentence in Pennsylvania.

Curiously, though, Simon's role in the Knox case appears to be limited to public relations in America, not legal strategy in Italy. Both of Amanda's Italian lawyers deny that he has any role in the appeal process. "*Simon non c'entro*—Simon doesn't enter into this," Luciano Ghirga told me emphatically, making it clear that neither he nor Carlo Dalla Vedova were ready to take a backseat to an American interloper. No one will confirm whether Simon is working pro bono, but sources close to the family say he volunteered to help them because he felt Amanda's lawyers weren't up to the job. David Marriott says that he has no idea whether Simon is being paid, although Marriott consults with him regularly about PR matters. Up to now, however, the two have had very different approaches to the case. Marriott has been fiercely critical of the Italian justice system and the individuals prosecuting the case. Simon, in his role as an independent TV commentator, told *Dateline* last year, "Speaking from experience, you have to be very careful when you try to be persuasive but not insulting, because you can't expect judges or jurists to receive your arguments or your evidence favorably when you've said terrible things about them." Perhaps the Knox family is finally ready to hear that advice.

THROUGHOUT THIS CASE, the mantra for pro-Amanda supporters has been that this was the "railroad job from Hell." When you consider the botched knife evidence, the shoddy police work, and the prosecutor's questionable past, it is easy to entertain the notion that Amanda Knox did not get a fair trial. But that doesn't mean she's innocent. Had the police done their jobs impeccably, and had all the extenuating circumstances fallen into place, Amanda Knox would probably still have been convicted of Meredith Kercher's murder. But nothing in this case ever made sense, and no one, it seems, played by the rules. Amanda Knox will always be remembered as someone who hung in the balance between sinner and saint, good and evil. And Meredith's murder will always be a mystery that was blurred by the headlines and lost in translation.

Acknowledgments

MEREDITH KERCHER'S MURDER was a heinous crime that robbed a young woman of her future and a unique family of their daughter. Her murder trial was a true media circus, but for those of us reporting from the center ring, it was also a profound experience. Though it is no consolation to her family, Meredith's memory will live on through all of the friendships that formed among those of us who covered her story.

Thank you to my editor and friend Lee Aitken, who guided this project, turning my on-the-ground dispatches into a real book. Lee invited me to join *The Daily Beast* by phone late one frigid night as I stood on the steps of the *enoteca* in Perugia. Through her I have had the most exhilarating adventure embarking on Tina Brown's pioneering journey in paperless media and fast book publishing. I am so lucky to be part of it and to work with so many smart people on the *Daily Beast* team. But I would never have been in Perugia in the first place if not for *Newsweek* magazine, for which I have worked since 1997. And I would not have received Lee's late-night call if my *Newsweek* bureau chief and trusted friend Chris Dickey had not suggested me for the part.

Very special thanks to Italo Carmignani for his willingness and generosity in sharing his reporting and knowledge of all things Perugian, which proved invaluable as a resource for this book.

Thank you to criminal lawyer Alessandra Batassa in Rome for always engaging on this story and for answering my many criminal-law questions.

Thank you to Andrea Vogt, whose verve as a reporter and friend has taught me more than a few things about integrity and about myself; to Sabina Castelfranco, whose honest friendship and genuine belief in Amanda's innocence have helped keep me in check; to Nick Pisa, whose untouchable reporting skills and wit make him the true *operatore*; and to Chapman Bell, whose dead-sprint enthusiasm made covering this story for so long so much more bearable. Others who have been important to this project, both as reporters and as friends, are Ann Wise of ABC, Marta Falconi of AP, Paul Russell of Fact TV, Massimo Mapelli of La7, and Alessandro Capponi of *Corriere della Sera*.

Big thanks to my sister Sherri for closely reading this manuscript so many times and for being such an honest critic, and to her, my parents, and my brother for not giving up on me when they easily could have. My deep appreciation goes to my dearest friends in Rome and Nairobi who have been so supportive, have helped with the kids, bought me my morning coffee, and listened to the gory details of Meredith's murder ad nauseam.

Last but not least, special thanks to Andrew for continuing to put up with my antics for all these years and to our sons Nicholas and Matthew, who aptly cringe when I mention "Perugia."